FROM GRIEF *to* GRATITUDE

BACK TO YOU!

MARION TURNER

Balboa Press books may be ordered through booksellers or by contacting:

Balboa Press
A Division of Hay House
1663 Liberty Drive
Bloomington, IN 47403
www.balboapress.com.au
1 (877) 407-4847

Print information available on the last page.

ISBN: 978-1-5043-1677-4 (sc)
ISBN: 978-1-5043-1678-1 (e)

Balboa Press rev. date: 02/15/2019

Contents

Dedication

To Ian, Cameron and Jude,
Thank you for loving so many versions of me.
I truly love every version of you too!

Acknowledgements

To my beautiful brother, Mostyn John Secombe

(05/04/1961 – 27/06/2007)

I want to thank you for all the joy, love and lessons we shared in our physical life together and for the lessons you continue to give me after your passing. I truly believe that it is through your passing that I have defined my purpose in life and know myself so much better than I ever thought I would. If you weren't so lovable, I would never have found myself in such a deep state of grief. You helped me find myself; I had to fall so low to find out that I never knew what I didn't know!

To my best friend and soul-mate, my wonderful husband Ian, my beautiful children Cameron and Jude.
Thank you for being my family, for loving me when I was not so lovable, for giving me the opportunities to grow and learn so I might heal myself and help others to do the same. Thank you for holding me close, I love you more than that!

To my much loved family – my parents Glenn and Elizabeth Secombe, my brother Gary and sister-in-law

Alison, nephew Matthew, niece Alana, sister-in-law Fiona and nephew Alex, beautiful cousins, aunts and uncles. I want to thank you all for being the wonderful loving family that you have always been, for sharing your memories of Mostyn, even when it's been painful, for your strength and love, you made the unbearable bearable.

To my "other" family – the Turners – too many to name, A family who has known deep grief on too many occasions and stays together through love and friendship - I love you all, thank you for being my family too!

To all my extended family and friends
Too many to mention by name, new friends, old friends, reconnected friends, You know who you are and I thank you for being in my life, I love you.

To my teachers
I wish to thank all those who have taught me in life, and most particularly for this part of my journey, Drs Ian and Ruth Gawler, Paul and Mia Bedson, Georgie Davidson and Paulette Watts. Thank you all, you have changed my life!

Last but by no means least, to all the *From Grief to Gratitude Workshop* participants
Thank you for your candour, your willingness to share your journey, your pain, your beliefs, I am indebted to you all. Thank you for trusting in the process and teaching me too.

Preface

"Every new beginning comes from some other beginning's end."
Seneca

I didn't know it at the time of course, but one phone call was going to change my life forever ...

On the 27th of June, 2007, my heart broke—a phone call broke my heart ...

This wasn't the first time I had lost someone dear to me, but it was the first time I felt myself fall to pieces. I had nowhere to go, I couldn't fix this, I had no history of dealing with this, how do I *do* this?

Therein lies the problem, it was never about *doing* anything, it was about *being* me and I didn't let myself just be, I made myself keep on doing. I had lost me.

At the time, my children were young, my daughter was seven and a half, my son had just turned four—and life went on—or did it? On reflection now, I find that *existence* went on, I survived in a physical sense and in a productivity sense too I guess, but I had definitely lost me. I started to try to claw my *self* back.

Looking back now, I see I needed to "come to my senses"; I had to get "out of my mind". These colloquialisms have a very real meaning to me, now I realise what they really mean; I needed to reconnect with my soul, my purpose—me.

There were twists and turns along the way, a long period of denial in which I had assumed that I had "dealt with" or "done my grieving" in the appropriate manner because life seemed to be going on okay. I even started a new physiotherapy practice on my return from the funeral and buried myself in work to get this new venture off the ground. My freelance medical editing work dried up (and I was kind of grateful as I found my attention to detail had begun to slip), but I was busy with my other physiotherapy work—in a private hospital and three aged care facilities.

Different things started to present themselves for my attention. Maybe they had done so in the past too but I was not ready to see them.

When the student is ready, the teacher will appear.

I was introduced to spiritual meditation by an acquaintance at the time, who later became my dear friend. Paulette waited for me at the gate when I dropped my son off at kindy (that's what we call pre-school in Adelaide) after returning from the funeral in Perth. She stopped and asked me if I was okay. For the first time I can remember in my "adult" life, I actually admitted to someone I barely knew that I was not. No, I was not okay, my brother had just passed away some 10 days before and I was not okay.

Paulette offered me a cup of tea and a chat at her house and I accepted—this was out of character for me, I am usually too busy to take up offers for a cuppa, particularly with someone I barely knew. Paulette is a deeply spiritual person—something I did not know prior to going to her house that morning, and although I had had my own experiences with premonitions and visions, I had never sought this type of guidance from anyone. Paulette told me my brother Mostyn was doing well, that a small, distinguished man in a suit had greeted him and helped him pass—he was waiting for him. I believe this to be my grandfather "Gar". I took comfort in this and wanted more. I even shared this information with my father and mother and found it brought them some peace as well. I was initially reluctant to tell them about this meeting because Dad had very strong views on "messing around with things you don't know about". I later introduced them to Paulette and they became friends, email buddies and mum and Paulette even became gym buddies. I began to attend Paulette's monthly meditation sessions—"Evenings with Gaia". These guided spiritual meditations were wonderful and during these sessions I always had interesting and peaceful travels, and I felt cared for by a higher source. I felt a sense of protection that I had not acknowledged before.

I've always been an avid reader, and my focus quickly turned to a different type of book, I pored over Diana Cooper, Doreen Virtue, and Neale Donald Walsch among others, and my perspective on the universe began to change. While I found comfort in these books, I began to question what I was doing with my life. What was I really meant to be doing?

As the years passed, my passion for meditation increased. I attended a Chronic Pain workshop, sponsored by WorkCover SA which, to my surprise, was meditation-based—unusual for a physiotherapy professional development session and an interesting choice of topic for a third party insurer. Georgie Davidson had been very active in bringing Mindfulness Meditation to the realm of traditional medicine in South Australia. This piqued my interest and I enrolled straight away. I remember remarking on that workshop that it was the only professional development course I had come away from feeling better than I did when I got there. After conferences and conventions, I would usually feel some enthusiasm for what I had learned but also quite drained and tired. I had never experienced this uplifting feeling and sense of peace after any workshop I had attended in the past. I found a different group of physiotherapists on this course and started to feel a connection with like-minded practitioners. Before the end of that weekend course, I had enrolled myself in Georgie's Mindfulness Based Stress Reduction course—for my personal and professional growth.

Georgie was wonderful, caring and supportive throughout the MBSR course and I found I loved the course/group feel (something I didn't usually participate in—I never considered myself to be a group type of person) and I knew from that moment I wanted to be able to teach this myself and help others. I deferred my enrolment into a Masters Degree in Physiotherapy to pursue meditation teaching.

My research on becoming a Meditation Teacher led me to the Gawler Foundation, what a revelation that was for me. I enrolled in Module 1 Teacher Training—Mindfulness-Based Stillness Meditation, and for me, the dots were finally connected. I felt a coming together of the spiritual meditation and the mindfulness meditation in this method devised by Dr Ian Gawler and Paul Bedson.

It was during this Module 1 course, wonderfully facilitated by Paul and Mia Bedson, that I discovered I was in fact still grieving! Yes, eight years on! Go figure – not me! I thought I had it all together! In October 2015, I experienced my grief and blockages on a physical level and IT ALL MADE SENSE! I became aware of my generalised state of "numbness". I was not feeling my emotions. Later, I realised the physical manifestation of my grief had already presented as illness in my body; I finally GOT IT! I experienced true stillness for the first time in this module!

I immediately began teaching the Gawler Foundation's 8-week Mindfulness-Based Stillness Meditation course on my return to Adelaide. I didn't give myself anytime to talk myself out of it, I found a venue and wrote my course manuals and had the course up and running in time for Term 4. The courses filled up quickly and I was so blessed to be able to have my mother on the course, I wanted to be able to help her heal too. Earlier, while on the Module 1 teacher training course I had intimated to my fellow participants that I couldn't possibly come back for Module 2 in the following year as my daughter would be completing her Year 12 studies then.

However, a sense of urgency came over me, I knew that I needed to be taught by Dr Ian Gawler, and I just had a feeling that he would be stopping his teaching soon. So, with the support of my family, I enrolled again and found myself back at the Gawler Foundation/ Yarra Valley Living Centre. Yes, my daughter was doing Year 12, but I was only away for a week - she managed extremely well and this trip allowed me to grow.

Module 2 – Guided Imagery and Contemplation Meditation was very enlightening for me. Again, wonderfully facilitated, this time by Drs Ian and Ruth Gawler, my blocks related to grief were highlighted to me once more and I was able to shift this through practice in the course. It was such a privilege to have been taught by Ian and Ruth and I am forever grateful that I chose to come along that year. I even got the same dormitory and bed I had in

Module 1 – I felt I had come home! It was during a contemplation type walking meditation through the labyrinth that another insight came to me.

Having yearned to be a writer since I can remember, I was always frustrated by not knowing what it was I should be writing. I had dipped my toes in around the edges and written for various music magazines, advising on injury prevention and later as a freelance proofreader and editor for medical journals and academic submissions and theses. But I knew I wanted to write something more, I just didn't know what.

As I neared the centre of the labyrinth, I was aware of others around me, and aware of my own purposeful steps, but I was mostly aware of my soul. I was walking in stillness, my mind cleared of thought when my insight came to me – *From Grief to Gratitude*. I absolutely knew then without a doubt that's what my teaching and writing purpose was about. I had had a real insight—a moment of absolute truth and clarity. I exited the labyrinth with a smile on my face, a sense of ease, peace and purpose swirling around inside me.

And so it was born, on my return from this teaching retreat, I began teaching the 4-week Gawler Foundation Guided Imagery course and I developed my own workshop – *From Grief to Gratitude*! I had finally come back to me!

I have immense gratitude for my amazing husband Ian and wonderful children Cameron and Jude for supporting me through this process, and to my teachers along the way: Paulette Watts, Georgie Davidson, Paul and Maia Bedson and Drs Ian and Ruth Gawler, and more recently my cousin Tracy Secombe, and her Soul Pleaser community.

The meditations from the Gawler Foundation that have been

used in this course have been used with very generous permission from Ian Gawler and Paul Bedson. I sincerely thank you both for your generosity and grace in allowing me to bring these insightful meditations to others. And to the readers, please, please avail yourself of the opportunity to spend time at a retreat or workshop with these amazing teachers.

My sincere hope for you reading this book is that you can reconnect with yourself, find your way back to you and that your journey may be quicker than mine!

From Grief to Gratitude is a course in practice and discovery, it guides you gently through finding the root of your issues—you may be surprised at what you find!

From Grief to Gratitude will give you a plan of action, a roadmap back to yourself—it seems so simple, *it is*, and it works! I am proof of this; my workshop participants are proof of this. May you find love for yourself and your life, may you find your purpose and start living again—right now!

With love and gratitude,
Marion

Chapter 1

Identifying Your Grief

"There is no grief like the grief that does not speak."
Henry Wadsworth Longfellow

My brother passed suddenly in the evening of June 27, 2007. Mostyn had moved to Western Australia with his family around two years before and had settled in well. He had a lovely house, was doing renovations and had a busy, stressful job as a proprietor/franchisee of a major national retail chain. He had let himself go a little (actually, not a little, quite a bit)—he had put on a lot of weight, he half-joked about applying for the Biggest Loser TV show (he had prior TV experience as a contestant on Perfect Match in the 1980's!). He still smoked cigarettes and drank too much alcohol but was determined to start to get fit again. He had returned home from playing squash with his good friend Ian – around 7.45pm WA time, showered and ate his dinner. He was tired and went to lie down at approximately 8.30pm. His left arm was achy (he was left-handed and it was only his second game of squash), so I can only guess that he dismissed this as being muscular. Mostyn passed away quietly and unexpectedly around 10 minutes later. His much-loved family found him blue and unresponsive; his 14 year-old stepson Alex had gone in to say goodnight and called to his mother Fiona. Fiona knew he was gone as soon as she entered the room. They worked to resuscitate him while they waited 20 minutes or so for the Paramedics to arrive. The Paramedics worked on Mostyn for around 10 minutes before calling the police and the coroner's van. Fiona could hear the oxygen from outside the room. Mostyn was 46 years old. Mostyn was my brother, my friend, and my challenge at times, but he was always in my heart. He was funny, often reckless, spontaneous, irritating, loving and ridiculous all at once. Mostyn passed at approximately 8.50pm in Western Australia (10.20 SA time).

On the June 27, 2007, I was preparing to go to my Body Balance™ class at a local gym in South Australia—the class was due to start at 7.30pm and I was running typically late. As I quickly washed the dishes after tea around 7.15pm (5.45pm WA time) I experienced crushing chest pain. It didn't last long and I put this down to indigestion—I had scoffed my spaghetti bolognaise quickly so I could make the class. At the end of the class, around 8.30pm (7pm WA time), I had another episode of the same pain—again it was short-lived. I stayed at the gym for a little longer and treated the Body Balance Instructor's neck before leaving and arriving home around 9.20pm (7.50pm WA time) after another episode of chest pain. I went to bed around 10.30pm (9.00pm WA time), not knowing my brother was gone.

At approximately 11.20pm (9.50pm WA time) my husband and I were woken suddenly by a phone call that would change our lives forever.

I jumped out of bed to answer the phone in our bedroom to hear Mum on the other end.

"Marion".

"Oh my God, what's happened to Dad?" I thought, Mum wouldn't ring at this time for a chat and she sounded dreadful. I don't think I answered out loud and she repeated herself.

"Marion, it's Mum" she said softly, "Mostyn's had a heart attack".

It took my breath away, "Where is he?" I asked.

"He's gone" Mum replied.

"Gone where?" I needed to know what hospital he was in!

"He died love".

Silence ...

"That's not fair, that's not right, that's not meant to happen." I felt like a ten year old. Dad was on the phone by now and I could hear him crying.

"Oh my God, "I'm coming over." I mouthed to Ian 'It's Mostyn'. He looked at me, he knew. I hung up the phone and sat on the bed and shook.

"He's dead, he's had a heart attack, he can't be dead ..." I don't know how long I sat there. I knew I had to see Mum and Dad and make sure they were okay. Ian was worried about me driving, it would only be a three-minute drive, we lived so near to each other! Ian held me while I cried, not the big sobs you would expect, they were for later I would discover. I was in disbelief. Ian cried too.

With two sleeping children in bed, Ian stayed home while I went to my parent's house – they didn't think I should drive the three minutes to their house either, so my older brother Gary and wife Alison picked me up on their way over! My niece Alana (19 years old) and nephew Matthew (22 years old) were in the car with Gary and Alison. My Auntie Wilma and Uncle Kevin arrived shortly after we did and the inevitable questioning and planning began, and so had our collective grief.

Of course, it's normal to grieve—grief causes acute sorrow and regret. Grief is a normal reaction to loss, that may be the loss of a loved one (as it was in my case), but it may be the loss of a relationship, a job, a circumstance, really anything you were once deeply attached to. Maybe it's the loss of a dream. How long should grief last? What's normal? Who really knows?

Those who don't allow themselves the time to grieve normally, or who grieve for a long time without any progress, roll on into complicated grief, which is also known as unresolved grief. So how do you know if you are suffering complicated grief? Here are some of the symptoms that can indicate the presence of unresolved grief according to the American Cancer Society:

- Continued disbelief in the death of a loved one
- Emotional numbness related to the loss
- Inability to accept the death
- Preoccupation with the loved one or how they died
- Intense sorrow and emotional pain, perhaps even intense anger or bitterness
- Inability to enjoy good memories of the loved one or the loss
- Self-blame for the death or loss
- Wishing to die to be with the loved one
- Excessive avoidance or reminders of the loss
- Continuous yearning and longing for the deceased or lost situation

- Loneliness, isolation, detachment from others, distrust of others
- Difficulty pursuing interests or planning for the future
- Hopelessness, emptiness, meaningless
- Loss of identity or purpose in life.

When grief remains unresolved, it becomes a problem. No matter the cause of your grief, unresolved or chronic grief leads to the same thing, your loss of self. Over time, unacknowledged grief turns into apathy, depression, procrastination, excessive busyness, loss of dreams, loss of sense of purpose and loss of self.

How do we get there, how do we end up in complicated grief? Personally for me, I think it was my innate talent for "soldiering on"—and I'm sure I'm not alone in this. My personal history reveals a number of times I have done this, where I have neglected my wellbeing and have landed in serious health difficulties with pneumonia, fatigue, autoimmune issues …

But, it was the only way I knew how to *do* it. I certainly wasn't expecting to lose a sibling, I had lost grandparents (all of them) but it seemed that there should be a natural order to life and death. I knew however that this wasn't so, I had lost friends who passed just after school, and in their thirties, and I had experienced the devastating loss of my beautiful baby niece Louise nearly eight years before and just like with the loss of Louise, I could feel myself silently screaming, "This just wasn't right; it wasn't fair!"

Death isn't really something we are generally comfortable talking about and we also feel uncomfortable talking to someone who is grieving—we don't know what to say. Maybe we don't need to say anything; maybe we can just listen and encourage our friends to talk when they're ready. On the flipside of that, I didn't know how to talk to other people about my grief either, and I felt I would be upsetting others by doing so.

After the funeral (or the divorce, or the relocation, or the shock of unemployment etc.), everyone else seems to get to move on. Yes, they are still sad and perhaps shocked and upset but their lives haven't been turned upside down. We think we have to just get moving as well and not let other people down, or make other people feel bad so we just pretend. We get up everyday, we smile, we don't feel, we don't accept, we soldier on! We keep on keeping on, that's what our society values. We think we think we feel, but we don't really. We know we feel sad, depressed, anxious, but we don't really explore those feelings, we will though, further on in this book.

In my instance, my husband suggested that perhaps I should see someone about my unhappiness, my depression. I was just "empty", like my soul had leaked out of the hole in my heart; I reluctantly accepted I was depressed. I had fought this suggestion in the past, for me it implied I had failed at coping and I was unaccustomed and averse to failure.

I discussed my emotional state with my doctor; I told her I just wasn't happy anymore. I wanted to be happy again, I missed my happy self. My wonderful doctor, who is very understanding but also quite pragmatic, informed me that no-one is really happy, not all the time anyway. I used to be, I was sure I used to be most of the time.

So I went along to a psychologist for around six sessions or so I think—for my depression—and I really didn't find a lot of joy in that process. I didn't have anything to take away, I needed some way to control this process, something to do …I still didn't realise

I was grieving. How could I be? This was five years later! The word grief didn't cross my mind.

So where do we start. What is grief?

It's really important to recognize that grief is a normal response to loss. In my opinion, if we honoured this more in our society, if we allowed people the time to grieve, we would have a healthier society. I know we don't honour grief as we should. My husband had issues at work with taking bereavement leave as Mostyn wasn't his "immediate family". My memory is that immediate family did not extend to spouse's siblings back them. Surely bereavement leave should extend to anyone we loved, regardless of blood ties.

A *From Grief to Gratitude* course participant has told me of issues at her workplace where she declined joining in a mother's day celebration as she had lost her mother some three months earlier. Her workplace management was unhappy and did not understand why she could not participate. The loss was months ago, why couldn't she just get on with it? I'm sure you have your own stories but really it gets down to a basic lack of understanding of the fundamental need we all have to be allowed to grieve and to be supported in our grief. There is no time limit, no right way or wrong way to do this.

Unfortunately our employers and government advisory departments seem to have a different view. My memory of the details of the leave options back in 2007 are sketchy and I've found it impossible to find them online now, to support my memory of it, but the recommendations for compassionate and bereavement leave in Australia in 2018, according to Fair Work Australia are

All employees are entitled to 2 days compassionate leave each time an immediate family or household member dies or suffers a life threatening illness or injury.

So, in Australia at least, we are sending a message that we should be back on track within two days! You don't even have to take the whole two day allowance continuously, you can split them up if you like – how very generous! So, we should be well enough to function, to operate heavy machinery, to make important decisions that affect the wellbeing of others, to sign contracts and whatever else you do at work. If you don't think you'll be fine in two days of the death of someone you love, you need to take other forms of leave, such as "sick leave" when you are going through this *normal* life process. If you have no sick leave, you need to use your holiday leave or take leave without pay! In the US 40% of workers get no paid time for bereavement leave.

Additional psychological assistance is often provided for those who have lost someone through traumatic situations – at the workplace, in a road accident, in a siege etc. but what about the people who experience loss through more "normal" means. Maybe the grief isn't related to a loss of a person, maybe it's related to the loss of a relationship, a job, or health. It's still grief, just the same.

In 2015, following her own experience with grief over the loss of her husband, Sheryl Sandberg, COO of Facebook, doubled the company's bereavement leave policy from 10 days to 20 days. Sandberg issued a challenge through a Facebook post for companies to change their bereavement and family leave policies with a number of firms increasing paid leave up to a month, some to eight weeks! Hopefully this is a social post that does go viral with public departments following their lead! Of course, it's not only work that goes on. Family life, looking after children all goes on too. There's precious little time to stop.

So what happens when we don't seem to be able to move on?

Complicated grief arises when we stay stuck in the past, when we haven't resolved our normal grief process. Maybe we're stuck in the blame game, blaming others for what we've lost, maybe we refuse to believe it's happened, maybe we've lost focus and direction in our lives, maybe we're engaging in addictive behaviours so we don't think about what's happened – alcohol, medication, drugs, poor food choices etc. … Maybe we don't realize we haven't processed our grief at all and our current behaviours are a consequence of the past but we don't know it yet.

We've most likely adopted our grieving behaviours from what's been modeled to us in our lives. I know as a 53 year old woman writing this now, I had never seen my father cry until my brother died. I remember the day my father's mother died but I have no recollection of seeing my father cry then (I'm sure he probably did, just not in front of the children – I was only around eight years old at the time). My Dad had lost his father a few years prior to losing his mother and I have little recollection of that time. I remember seeing my mother cry twice—once when her father died when I was around 23 years old and many years later when her friend Joan died. Life seemed to just go on after the funerals and Mum and Dad seemed to just go back to work and get on with life. That's how I saw it through my eyes. As a young child, I was not allowed to attend the funerals. I think my first funeral was my grandfather's (my mother's father) when I was 23 years old. So I never really felt I got to say goodbye to anyone either until that time. I learned that to be successful at grief, you just had to get on with it. Looking back on it now, it seems so weird, I had seen dead bodies before this time, I had dissected the bodies of the generous souls who donate their bodies to science at University when I was 17 years old and I had walked in on patients who had passed in the hospital, but I had never been to a funeral.

What have you seen modeled in your family regarding grief when you were a child? We took our children to Mostyn's funeral – they loved him too and it gave them a chance to experience their grief and to say goodbye. Comments were passed, I remember my Dad thinking that I would be the only one flying over to Perth for the funeral, he seemed surprised that we would all be coming. I also overheard some remarks at the funeral about children being present.

You may be wondering where gratitude fits in with all of this? And what is gratitude? Gratitude is simply being thankful - and to be truly thankful and to feel gratitude, you need to be operating in the present. The importance is in where our attention is lying - when we are grieving, we are locked in the past, when we are experiencing gratitude, we are being present.

Even if we can't flick a switch and jump to being happy and grateful, we can start to learn to practice gratitude and shift our focus to the present. But how do we even start operating in the present? What tools do we have that we can use to shift our focus to the present?

And how do we know if we are really present? If you find yourself saying things like "I can't wait until ..." or "Remember when ..." or you are constantly looking at your phone when someone is talking to you, or you are thinking of what to cook for dinner while you're driving the car or talking over someone else while they are talking to you, then you are not present! You are not present when you are reading a book and you can't remember what you read, you are not present when you have been watching the news and can't remember what was on. You are not present when you are not paying attention to the now.

We have several tools we can use to get ourselves focused and engaged in the present moment. We can use them to practice and re-learn where we want our awareness to rest. My favourite tools are grounding and mindfulness. Mindfulness can be used as a tool, but with practice, mindfulness becomes a way of being, rather than a tool to use.

Simply understanding and experiencing grounding is an important tool in my arsenal for settling myself down and bringing myself to the present moment. What is grounding you may ask? Grounding sounds like a nebulous concept until you understand the simplicity of it all. It's really just connecting with your environment. It also incorporates mindfulness because you are paying attention to what is happening right now. For some it is about centering your soul in your body and connecting both your soul and your body to the earth. For many people this is a difficult concept to grasp and that's okay. If you don't consider yourself a spiritual type of person that's okay, this works for you anyway, just approach it from a practical point of view. The simplicity of grounding for me is to simply sit in a chair, feet on the floor (I like bare feet but it can be done with shoes on), feeling the pressure of the feet on the floor, the buttocks on the chair, the back resting against the back of the chair, the hands on the thighs, feeling the connection between the hands and the thighs, the head resting directly above the shoulders. Adopting an open and upright posture gives a feeling of strength and courage to face the world and the feeling of the body against the physical environment gives a sensory connection to the present. For me, grounding is a more physical sensation-based activity than a full mindfulness meditation. It is quick and easy to use to reset and reconnect yourself to the present moment.

Mindfulness is a simple practice, that is profound in its applications and benefits and everyone can practice this. Jon Kabat-Zinn describes mindfulness as "non-judgmental awareness of the present moment." He is the founder of the Stress Reduction Clinic at the University of Massachusetts Medical School and in 1979 he established the Mindfulness-Based Stress Reduction program for the chronically ill and through his teachings, Mindfulness Based Stress Reduction programs are operating in over 720 hospitals and clinics around the world.

Mindfulness is the ability to notice, to be aware, to accept the presence of what is around you at the time without passing judgement either way – not reacting, not judging – simply noticing. When you notice yourself commenting internally, you simply allow the thought to pass and return to whatever it is you are being mindful of. Simply noticing that you are being distracted is being mindful! We are not perfect; it is normal for our minds to be distracting, and that's okay. Please don't judge yourself harshly with negative self-comments; just allow the distraction to pass. Mindfulness meditation is grounding too!

"Do not dwell in the past, do not dream of the future,
concentrate the mind on the present moment."
Buddha

So let's try a mindfulness meditation – I particularly enjoy mindfulness that builds into stillness meditation – and I have included two versions – Mindfulness-Based Stillness Meditation – written by Paul Bedson and Stillness Meditation written by Dr Ian

Gawler. I personally enjoy mixing meditation up a little, so I am happy to give you options to try.

You can practice these meditations by having someone read them to you – you can record this on your phone while they do read it to you. Or alternatively, you can record them yourself. My website (marionturner.com) will allow you access to my recorded versions of these meditations, if you contact me by email, I can provide you a link to listen to these. Both Ian Gawler and Paul Bedson have recorded meditations on websites (Ian Gawler at iangawler.com and Paul Bedson at gawler.org) and both have meditation CDs for purchase from gawler.org. Dr Ian Gawler founded the Gawler Foundation and has assisted thousands of people with cancer with his meditation courses, retreats and some hospital-based programs. Paul Bedson is a counselor and meditation teacher who has been working in the field of mind-body medicine for many years.

Mindfulness-Based Stillness Meditation (Paul Bedson)

Gently close your eyes and settle into your body. Take a moment now to adjust your posture … Sit with an upright and open posture. Now, in your own way, take a few moments to relax your body … Take three slow, deep conscious breaths and as you breathe out feel your muscles softening and loosening. Relaxing, awake and alert.

Allow your breath to find its own depth and rhythm now … to just breathe itself.

Now become aware of the space before your closed eyes … it's like a field of darkness … perhaps there are some muted shapes or colours … just simply resting your attention there.

With relaxed eyes and a soft gaze. (Pause)

Now bring your attention to any sounds coming to you from outside (pause) ... or inside the room ... just simply listening ... with a gentle curiosity ... (pause)

Let the sounds come and go ... (pause)

Allow the sounds to call your attention into the present moment ... just listening.

Now as you bring your awareness to your breath, notice the feeling of the breath ... as you breathe in ... and as you breathe out ... feel the air moving over your nostrils ...

Feel the slight movement of your chest and your belly ... rising with the in-breath, sinking with the out-breath.

Perhaps there is even a gentle sound with your breathing ... just your natural breathing ... follow each breath. (Pause)

Next, bring your awareness down to your feet ... Move your awareness through your feet ... notice any sensations in your feet ... just feel them ... feeling into your toes ... your heels ... the surface of your feet ... all through the feet ... and as you feel into your feet, feel the flow of your breath ... simply coming and going ... just watching ... quite effortlessly. (Pause)

Now bring your awareness up to your hands ... rest your attention on your hands ... feel the touch of your hands against your thighs ... your fingers touching each other ... notice that subtle sense of aliveness through your hands ... explore all the small sensations around and through your hands. (Pause)

Now bring your awareness to your shoulders ... Notice the feeling in the muscles of your shoulders ... the base of your neck ... a pressure or a tingling ... Just feel it ... simply noticing ... And as you feel into the muscles of your shoulders ... feel the flow of your breath ... simply being aware of the breath. (Pause)

Now, as you are aware of the space before your eyes, become aware of any sensations in and around your eyes ... move your attention through your eyebrows ... and across your forehead ... notice whatever sensations are there ... as you feel through the eyes and across the forehead, feel the flow of your breath ... just resting in the awareness.

Now, with a willingness to get in touch with how you are feeling inside, bring your awareness to your centre ... the feeling line of the body ... feeling into the throat ... feeling into the centre of the chest ... feeling into the solar plexus ... and feeling into the belly ... resting your attention along the whole feeling line of your being ... Keep the feelings company, with curiosity and compassion ... just simply being aware ... And as you notice the feelings in your centre, feel the flow of your breathing.

Open your awareness to the whole body ... notice whatever sensations are coming into your awareness at this particular moment ... perhaps the awareness of the space in front of your eyes ... perhaps the feeling of the breath ... If any thoughts come to your awareness, just let them come and go ...watch the thoughts coming and going. And notice the background of stillness ... the background across which the thoughts travel ... just noticing whatever comes and goes ... just noticing ... being aware of that still and silent presence ... simply resting in that stillness.

(Long Pause)

If you notice your attention wandering or becoming caught up in a stream of thought ... simply bring your attention back to the next breath ... being aware of the feeling of the breath again ... and notice the sounds, your feet resting on the floor, the feeling line through your centre ... as you rest your attention in the space in front of the eyes.

(Long Pause)

Now as we come towards the end of this, allow your breathing to become a little stronger ... perhaps a deeper breath or two ... start to reactivate your body by moving your fingers and toes … have a stretch … and when you are ready slowly open your eyes.

Stillness Meditation (Dr Ian Gawler)

So let's begin by taking a few moments to adjust our bodies and settle into our posture … back just as upright as your body is comfortable … feet flat on the floor, a little apart … then you might like to lean back a little, and feel the support … from the back of the chair … hands resting on the thighs, or simply cupped in the lap … just notice what is most comfortable for you… and then, when you are ready … you might like to join me for a few moments … and let your eyes close gently …

Now, just be curious to notice the sounds you can hear right now … Notice any sounds coming to your awareness from outside of this room … aim to simply notice them … have the intention of letting go of any judgement … "I like this sound … hope it continues …" "Or, I do not like this sound … hope it stops …" just simply noticing … with a gentle curiosity …

And then bringing your attention more particularly into this room, this space we are in … and noticing any sounds coming from within the room itself … again, just noticing … free of any judgement or commentary … simply aware of the sounds … the pure sounds … pure awareness …

And then bringing your attention more particularly once again to your own body, and listening closely … maybe you can notice the subtle sounds of the breath … breathing in … and breathing out … and as you do bring your attention more to the breath, notice too, the movement in the body as you are breathing in … and breathing out … so being aware that as we are breathing in, we are breathing in … as we are breathing out, we are breathing out …

And as you continue to hold your attention on the breath … you will probably notice that each time that you do breathe out, there is just a natural feeling of letting go a little ... it is just a natural thing ... that as we do breathe out, we tend to let go a little, to relax a little ... So without making any more or less of this ... simply noticing ... each time we breathe out ... relaxing a little ...

And at the same time, notice how as you do breathe out, the outbreath tends to taper away ... to become longer ... finer ... subtler ...

So breathing out ... letting go ... relaxing a little and the outbreath becoming longer ... finer ... subtler ...

And when the outbreath is completed ... often there is a pause ... and then aim to simply allow the in-breath to come back in of its own accord ... breathing out ... the outbreath longer ... finer ... subtler ... that feeling of letting go ... relaxing a little ... then a pause ... and simply allowing the in-breath to come back in of its own accord ... quite effortlessly ... effortlessly ...

And now, it might help to take your attention to that point between the eyes, a little into the forehead ... and notice there what is like a still, quiet centre ... a point of stillness ... maybe you notice it more particularly in that area behind the closed eyelids ... so just holding your attention now lightly on that point of stillness ... and it is almost as if you can merge into that stillness ... relaxing ... releasing ... just simply letting go ... quite effortlessly ... effortlessly ... letting go ... letting go ... resting in that stillness for a few moments ...

BIG GAP

And if at any stage you do notice your mind wandering or becoming distracted ... gently bring your attention back to that quiet space ... that point of stillness ... relaxing ... releasing ...

Merging ... melting ... simply resting in that stillness now for a few moments ... quite effortlessly ... effortlessly ... letting go ... letting go ...

BIG GAP

That's good ... good ... good ... when you are ready now ... just let your eyes gently open once again ...

Please do perform the meditation before you move on to the next step. The clarity you have following meditation will help you in identifying the cause of your grief. To prove this to yourself, you can try the journaling activity prior to the meditation, and then again after the meditation and compare the writing between the two. Both of these meditations are wonderful, grounding, settling meditations that bring clarity and peace, they are a wonderful way to start your day!

Your personal journey from Grief to Gratitude starts now! Of course, we could be grieving the loss of more than one thing from our lives at once. Just take it slowly and focus on one situation at a time, more may be revealed to you as you progress through the exercises. The reason for this book not holding the space for you to enter your answers directly in it, is that you can continue to use this method over and over again for other situations should you require.

Yes, I too have been guilty many times of starting to answer questions and then not finishing all of the exercises and simply reading forward. If you are serious about change in your life, I urge you to stop and take the time to do each exercise. I would love to hear from you that actually did the exercises in this book. If you do and would like to share that with me, please do so, you can contact me through my website www.marionturner.com or my Facebook page "Humanity Matters Always". You don't have to tell me anything about what you have discovered or your personal journey, although I would love to hear that, if you like, you can just tell me that you committed to the exercises.

I implore you, I urge, I beg you to do them, to do it for yourself, for your family, for your friends, for your life, for your community, for our planet. If every one of us is trying to be our best self, the world can't help but be a better place. And before you say it, yes, you do have time, you have the time to read my words, so spend some time writing your own. There is no race to finish within a certain time frame, but my experience tells me if you are on a roll, keep going! You will have your action plan for change in no time.

We do this workshop live in a weekend so you can aim to do that too if you wish. Alternatively, if you spend an hour a day on this, you should have this done in two to four weeks. What a great return on investment you will have when you come out the other side with purpose, joy and peace.

Hints for this process:

1. Use a notebook or journal that is dedicated to *From Grief to Gratitude* alone – don't mix it up with anything else.
2. Write in a notebook instead of using a computer – hand written words can have more impact for you.
3. Use a lovely pen - enjoy the writing process.
4. Find a quiet space to write, allow yourself 30 minutes or so for each writing exercise where you can allow your writing to flow uninterrupted..
5. Put the phone away, turn the TV off, and don't answer the door.
6. As you write, please don't edit yourself, allow the words to flow and don't avoid writing things for fear of someone else seeing it, this is your work and you can protect it if you need to. It's important to get it out.

Workbook Activity

Identifying Grief:

1. What is the cause of your grief? Giving this a title is likely to be enough of an answer here but you may wish to write the story of it too, that can be quite cathartic in itself. You may have a list of things you are grieving – feel free to write it all down, writing how it makes you feel can be helpful too. If you have more than one incident you are grieving over, pick one to work on the first time through the book. You may find others may dissolve as you do this.
2. Describe yourself before grief – a description of what you used to do, who you spent time with, any hobbies, sports, social, recreational activities, work you were involved in. What your family was like, what your health issues, fitness, nutrition and sleep were like, and what desires and goals you had for your future. What did you want in your life?
3. Describe yourself after grief – describe what you do now, who you spend time with now, any hobbies, sports, social, recreational activities, work you are involved in. What is your family like now, describe any health issues you face now if any, your fitness, nutrition and sleep patterns and the desires and goals you hold for the future now.
4. How do you know you're grieving?

   a) Are there any behaviours you would like to change? Consider alcohol, drugs, medication, social withdrawal, exercise, food, busyness, laziness, procrastination …

   b) Are there any feelings you would like to change? Maybe consider despair, hopelessness, sadness …?

Identifying your behaviours and feeling states can help highlight if we are still grieving, sometimes we stop caring for ourselves the way we used to, and we most likely experience less joy in our lives than we used to. Perhaps we're just less invested in our lives when we're grieving!

Please don't move on to Chapter Two until you've taken the time to discover some things about yourself. And don't be afraid to be honest, you've shown up now because you know something is not right, this life is not working for you right now. You have the power and strength to change this and it's really not that hard. It's about taking the time for you, the time to honour yourself which then allows you to honour this life of yours.

Chapter 2

Who Have You Become?

"Not until we are lost do we begin to understand ourselves."
Henry David Thoreau

Change is inevitable following a traumatic loss. In fact, we change a little every day, whether we are growing in self confidence from successes, becoming more compassionate as we help our friends and families through their troubled times, or maybe we become more withdrawn, bitter or cynical when we've been hurt. It's hard to stay on track, but who's to say what our track is and what it's meant to be. We have free will, we have choices, but the problem I found was that I didn't really have the energy to make inspired choices, instead I chose to just keep on keeping on! I was simply existing; I was not living. I would get up in the morning, I would look after the children, take them to school; I was invested in their lives but not in my own. I was more invested in the lives of my patients than I was in mine because that too was a form of escape. That was a way to ignore what was going on (or not going on) in my own life. And I knew how to help them, I could assess and see what was wrong and I had solutions for them! Unknowingly I was grieving the person I used to be as well but I guess I just assumed this was it! This was how I was now after the loss of my brother, I mean, only a heartless person wouldn't have changed from something as big as that! Oh, the losses that followed his as well, beautiful friends passing away—we must have had at least five funerals of young people (well under 60, one a young teen), within the following two years! I looked back on the school friends who had passed away since we left school – the first was only 20 years old, then there were more. For goodness sake, two of my friends had become widows in their 30's. This wasn't the life I had envisioned when we were at school. Another friend had lost her disabled son. Our beautiful niece passed away at 12 days old while I was pregnant with my daughter! I was married to a beautiful man who had lost his father when he was only 16 years old ...

So I guess I lost faith in the world, in the premise that God was loving and nurturing, it was all so cruel! Did God exist? Was there really a higher spiritual loving presence? These were all such good people! So, I toughened up! That was my innate defense mechanism, I covered myself in an armour of concrete. Yes, I was still compassionate towards everyone else, I felt their pain I just didn't make time for myself. I didn't feel mine, I didn't have empathy for me! I had forgotten what I loved to do, and when I did remember, I couldn't be bothered. I thought I would get back to doing things but I didn't. I found myself caught up in the busyness of life so I didn't have to try to get back to me, it was all too hard! I didn't talk to my family about my grief because I didn't want to upset them! Looking back now, I feel I denied others an opportunity to talk to me about Mostyn's passing rather than protecting them. I've heard others tell similar stories in my workshops, that they avoided talking with other loved ones about their losses, that they didn't want to upset others, that they just assumed this was what life was going to be like moving forward.

I sort of apologise for telling my story and then I don't—I think it's important for you to sense the vulnerability of someone else, that we're having a conversation, and that you are not alone in "feeling different", that you don't feel how you once did. Please take time to stop and think about yourself as you read through this book, just mark where you're up to in the book and take the time to think.

This whole process in *From Grief to Gratitude* restores your connection with humanity as you begin to understand, accept and allow others' behaviours and feelings to be as normal as yours, and yours to be as normal as theirs. It's when we stop this feeling of separation, the "me and everyone else", the "us and them" that we begin to restore our connection with humanity and ourselves in a healthier way. We need to know that this grieving process is normal, we need to know that death is a normal part of life, that we will all experience this and our death will affect others around us. We need to start talking about things. We need to know what other peoples' wishes are, we need to keep communicating with our loved ones and we need to not be afraid to ask the big questions. If they don't offer us the information, how can we possibly know? Why isn't there a handbook in everyone's house called My Last Wishes where all the details down to "How I want to be dressed for my funeral" are laid out simply—so grieving family members don't have to make those decisions and then second-guess themselves or beat themselves up for getting it wrong. For all kinds of loss we experience, communication is key. It's through discussion that we grow in understanding and compassion. We feel our connection with others and have the chance to adopt a different view of our situation. We don't feel as alone, we don't necessarily blame ourselves for things we have or haven't done. We begin to understand how others feel too, that through our loss, even though our individual stories may be different, we are connected.

Now is the time to sit and reflect and acknowledge who you are now. Not who you want to be, not who you used to be, but who you are right now.

This can be an exposing exercise, so take your time but please make sure you do this. If you don't do this, you will be starting a journey without a starting point. How can you get directions to get somewhere if you don't know where you are right now? It's like asking for directions on your phone, but not allowing the phone to access your location! Pretty pointless really! So turn on your inner location services setting and get started. Meditation can help you increase your awareness of where you're located now!

Try this meditation on Mindfulness of Emotions first, and don't be discouraged if you find this a little difficult, it's likely you haven't spent a lot of time being aware of how you really feel emotionally. This centering meditation allows you to become aware of the physical sensations in the centre-line of your body, these physical sensations are connected to our emotions. You know how you get "butterflies" in your stomach when you're excited or nervous, or a "lump in your throat" when sad, or a "gut feeling" when something is wrong? We even incorporate the acknowledgement of these sensations in our language, but oddly enough, we don't spend time daily or routinely, checking in with how we are feeling.

This is a gentle practice that is different every time you do it, so please don't set up any expectations, just go with the flow, go with the flow with every meditation included in this book. One of the key things to remember about meditation is that there is no right or wrong way to meditate, there is not an end goal you are striving for, it is a process, a way of being; that is all. Maybe you think you experience your feelings too much, but in my experience with teaching this meditation to others, we don't generally connect the physical sensation to the emotional experience and most people tend to ignore or deny their true feelings.

Rumi's famous poem "The Guest House" invites us to feel all our emotions, to greet them warmly, to live in the present moment and accept what we are feeling right now, and to learn from our experiences.

The Guest House

This being human is a guesthouse.
Every morning a new arrival.

A joy, a sadness, a meanness,
some momentary awareness comes
as an unexpected visitor.

Welcome and entertain them all!
Even if they're a crowd of sorrows,
who violently sweep your house
empty of its furniture.
Still, treat each guest honourably.
He may be clearing you out
for some new delight.

The dark thought, the shame, the malice,
meet them at the door laughing,
and invite them in.
Be grateful for whoever comes,
because each has been sent
as a guide from beyond.

Rumi

Centering/Feelings Meditation (Paul Bedson)

Assume an upright and open posture, close the eyes.

Pay attention to the screen of darkness in front of your eyes, slightly up at the level of the eyebrows …

Pay attention to the sounds outside the room, then the sounds inside the room. Just listening without judgement or attachment …

Now take the attention down to the feet, feel the sensations of pressure where your feet touch the floor, then feel the subtle sense of aliveness in the feet, a subtle tingling, pressure of light pulsing …

Allow your breathing to flow naturally.

Now with the intention to check-in with how you are feeling, bring awareness to your throat, feel into it, explore the sensations – subtle or stronger. If thoughts or memories come to mind, allow them to come but bring your attention back to the sensations in the throat. (Pause)

Let your breathing flow. Now bring attention to the centre of your chest, feeling for any sensations, a slight pressure, ache, hardness or resistance to your breathing, or perhaps it feels soft or comfortable. Explore the feeling sensations with a non-judgemental curiosity. (Pause)

Now bring awareness to your solar plexus [your upper belly]. Explore the sensations, tightness, a contraction, shakiness, numbness, softness …

whatever sensations you find. Just accept them with a non- judgemental curiosity. (Pause)

Now bring your awareness down to the belly, around the navel and behind the navel. No need to analyse whether the sensations come from a physical cause or an emotional cause. They affect each other. Explore all the sensations. (Pause)

Now broaden the awareness to include the whole feeling line of your being: the throat, the chest, the solar plexus and belly. Keep the feelings company with curiosity and compassion, just sitting with whatever feelings are there.

Now open your awareness to include your breathing, the sensation in your feet, the sounds and, of course, the awareness of the 'silent observer', the 'still presence' which notices sounds, sensations, thoughts and feelings.

As you practice this more, you will find it easier. When I first attempted this meditation I was unable to feel any physical sensations in my centre-line below the level of my chest, I was numb. I experienced this in my initial meditation-teaching module with this exact meditation. Later on, I experienced it again in an invocation meditation, where I could not direct light through my body past the level of my chest. It made sense to me, in fact, these two experiences were my insight and my confirmation that I was stuck in grief! I was stuck at the level of my heart, and through the practice of this meditation, I gradually became aware of sensations below my heart, I allowed the acceptance and the energy to flow through me, I allowed myself to let go. I'm not sure if I had dissociated from my feelings or I was suppressing them, the end result was the same to me as I really wasn't experiencing them fully in a physical sense and most likely that results in an incomplete emotional experience too! I'm not a psychologist and I don't profess to know the difference between dissociation and suppression but I'm feeling the end result may be similar.

Now it came as no surprise to me that holding on to my grief, concentrating energy in this area for so long, manifested change in my body physically. I developed oesophageal ulcers—I was initially investigated in the Emergency Department for cardiac issues on a couple of occasions (which was a little frightening, given my family history). At other times, I experienced this pain and didn't present to the Emergency Department because I was tired and I'd had enough. I simply thought if it's my time, "I'll go now, I'm done." This is a particularly difficult thing for me to say, knowing that my children, my parents, my family and friends will likely read this book. Yes, at times I thought that was the easiest solution – to surrender my life. Oh my God! As I say this now, I cannot believe that was me feeling this but I was exhausted. I just didn't want to continue with my life that way.

I am so very happy to say that is not me any more, and I am excited to live my life now, I am curious about myself, I am keen to see what's around the next corner for me. I am more resilient in an accepting kind of way. That seems to be a contradiction, but by the end of this course, you'll know what I mean.

So if you feel you've lost touch with your emotions, maybe you have. Maybe it's a protective mechanism, maybe you're exhausted, and maybe it's a combination of the two. But you know what, I know you want to feel better because you're actually reading this book. Don't lose faith, this has worked for me and if it's worked for someone, it's possible! You may have noticed the areas we concentrated on in this meditation are the same as the chakras. I love to see the science and the spiritual connect and for me, it felt my energy flow was blocked and I was able to restore this through mindfulness of emotions meditations. The chakras unite the three elements of your being, your mind, body and soul. When the energy is flowing through these fully, you radiate energy, peace and happiness. When the energy is blocked, you feel tired, lethargic and lost. So while this meditation may seem the most difficult to get a handle on, please practice this regularly to restore your mind, body and spirit connection. This can make your energy work for you, not against you as I feel it was doing in my case – manifesting in disease.

Workbook Activity

Using your notebook, write about yourself now. You may like to just think about yourself in general and let your writing flow, many people find this difficult, particularly when it is something they haven't considered for a long time.

You may find it easier to follow these guidelines to get yourself started.

These are ideas that are useful to consider, and if you like, it may be easier to start with a scale of 0-10 where 0 is least and 10 is most. For example:

Happiness/contentment

---

0 1 2 3 4 5 6 7 8 9 10

Comments:

Draw a scale for each section. Leave some space under the scale to write some comments, once you let yourself think and reflect, it's amazing how much can come to the surface. You can ask the opinions of others after if you like, but try and discover yourself first. I find people are happy to ask others for their opinions as it stops them having to think too much about themselves. You can use the comments section to compare yourself to how you were before the event as well, as it's likely this comparison will come up in your mind as you're completing the task. Don't be too hard on yourself but do take the time to do this. You are switching on your location services right now and finding your starting point.

Where do you sit on the scale for:

Happiness/contentment

How often do you find pleasure or contentment in your day? As I've said before, it's normal to experience a range of emotions and happiness and contentment should be a part of that. Maybe you are experiencing it, but just taking notice of the unhappiness?

0 = never experiencing contentment or pleasure, 10 = most of the day spent in contentment.

Energy

How energetic do you generally feel from getting up in the morning to going to bed? Are you dragging yourself around to get things done, or do you jump out of bed with a spring in your step?

0 = can't even get out of bed – lying around most of the day, 10 = never running out of energy.

Procrastination

How often do you look for excuses to put off or delay things you need to get done? Do you put off the "difficult tasks" and do the easy things first until you've run out of time to do the harder ones? Perhaps make a list of things you've been putting off. Fear of failure can be a reason for procrastination, but lack of planning, order and commitment are other factors worth considering. Procrastination is not laziness. Laziness is an unwillingness to get moving and doing things. Procrastinators tend to be quite busy doing lots of other things, just not the most important ones – they often start projects and don't finish them, or they'll do it tomorrow—they generally will get things done by a deadline if it has to be done but if there's no deadline, it's unlikely to get pushed up the ever growing list.

0 = never procrastinate, always tackling the most important things first, 10 = never get anything done

Motivation

How much desire do you have to do things and get things done? Motivation is generally the driver that spurs people on to completing tasks, to achieving success and establishing habits. Do you jump out of bed, hankering to take on the world? Or do you drag yourself out of bed through obligation to get things done for other people? Do you care about the outcome of getting things done?

0 = no activity, you don't do anything! 10 = always hankering to get things done.

Direction/goals/dreams

Do you know where you're going in life? Do you have a vision for your future that you're excited about creating? Do you have goals—measurable goals that you are working towards? Have you forgotten what your dreams were?

0 = no dreams, ambitions, passions, 10 = regularly reviewing goals, recording dreams, vision boards etc.

Love

How much love do you feel for your family and friends? (We'll get to you later!).

Do you experience feelings of deep affection, interest and pleasure in other people, in hobbies, in pets, in humanity?

0 = no interest or affection for others, 10 = overflowing with love

Intimacy

You can be intimate with your partner or others around you without it having to be a sexual relationship, however this is an important consideration too. Has your sexual relationship changed? But remember, intimacy also includes how personal you are with someone else, how comfortable you are in revealing your feelings and thoughts, your rapport and attachment with others, how close and comfortable are you in your relationships. Perhaps you might want to divide this section into two parts.

0 = no intimacy, not close to anyone at all 10 = very intimate with at least one person in your life, who you can tell anything to, have a strong physical connection as well if you have a partner

Connectedness with others

It's easy to think you are connecting well with people because you are busy doing things for them, but until you understand how you are not connecting with yourself, not understanding that what you are going through is normal and part of the whole human experience, you are not really connected with others. When you see yourself as isolated and alone, when you see "them" getting on with things and you're not, it sets up an "us and them" scenario, which by definition is disconnected. Perhaps it's seeing other loved ones moving on and you're not, "They just don't get it", "they didn't love him as much as me" you are being judgemental.

0 = I'm completely alone and different, 10 = I understand and feel I am part of the shared human experience and understand and accept other people's suffering and joy as much as I do mine.

Self-worth

How confident are you in your abilities, how highly do you value yourself? Do you feel worthy or confident to take your place amongst others? Do you feel less worthy than others? Do you feel worthy of love and success?

0 = unworthy 10 = I am amazeballs

Health

How would you rate your health on a scale of 0-10.

0 = dead 1 = near death, 10 = you couldn't get any healthier.

Medications

Are you taking medications you were not taking pre-grief? Are you happy doing so and being on these?

0 = no new medications (or no difference since onset of grief), 10 = lots of new medications – related to emotional well-being, nutritional neglect, cardiovascular issues and more

Mood

How labile are your moods – do they switch around quickly? Do you find yourself angry, irritable, unpleasant, critical, disappointed, or sad? Or are you generally pleasant, affable, kind?

0 = don't come near me, not sure how the wind blows today, 10 = stable and pleasant all of the time

Weight

How happy are you with your weight at present? Has it changed much since the grief process started?

0 = very unhappy with weight 10 = very happy with weight

Nutrition

What choices have you been making with your nutrition, do you put effort into eating wisely, providing your body with good nourishment? Are you turning to the quickest options because you're busy? Are you taking time to plan what you and your family are eating?

0 = no thought into nutrition, just eating whatever is around or quick to throw together? 10 = menu planner, concerted effort with nutrition

Exercise

How often do you take time out to exercise? This doesn't have to be a gruelling gym session, maybe it's a 30 minutes walk daily? Maybe it's a morning yoga or stretching ritual? What are you doing for yourself with exercise?

0 = no planned exercise, 10 = regular exercise routine

Sleep

How well are you sleeping? Does it take a long time to get to sleep at night? Do you wake at 3am and can't get back to sleep for an hour or two, only to fall into a deep sleep and then be woken by the alarm? Are you falling asleep during the day?

0 = no sleep (which is very unlikely), 10 = perfect sleep – straight to sleep, uninterrupted and waking refreshed.

Other (there may be something else you want to consider)

In Chapter 1, we wrote about things we *did* before grief and the things we do now. This is more of an exploration of how we *were* emotionally and physically before grief and how we are now. This is more of a "being" exploration than the "doing" one in Chapter 1. Now, it's really important that you do this as a practice of identification and acceptance, and not take this as an opportunity to beat yourself up because "you've let yourself go" or "you've turned into an ice queen" etc., this is the opportunity for change and I can absolutely guarantee you, you will view yourself more harshly than anyone else does (especially those who love you). Please take the time to really consider these questions and answer honestly.

Finally, give yourself a big pat on the back for doing this one, yep it's not easy and you just did it. Just in case you haven't done it yet – don't move on until you have. Don't read on and think you'll get back to it later, DO IT NOW. Remember that procrastination scale?

"Procrastination is the thief of time."
Edward Young

Chapter 3

Someone You Need To Meet

"Who in the world am I? Ah, that's the great puzzle."
Lewis Carroll (Alice in Wonderland)

So here are some of the big questions we all face in life; who am I? Who am I supposed to be? Am I allowed to change? What is my purpose? Why can't I work myself out? Why do I seem to have great advice for everyone else and none for myself?

Any of these sound familiar? Our lives become busy and full of things—things to do, things to take care of, things to wash, things to clean, things to attend, things to organise, things to remember. Sometimes we give our love and attention to material things—which is crazy, these things can't love us back! We need to start to shift our attention to meaningful parts of our lives.

Of course some of these "things" are essential for us to live in a society, to maintain our health and hygiene and allow our families to run smoothly. But where in that planner or calendar of daily activities is the time blocked out for our self-care? When did we last really sit down and take stock of our lives, remember our dreams, and plan for some adventure and excitement. Often after the loss of a loved one, a relationship, a job etc., we just carry on with the mundane things in our lives because we can manage to do that. We tread the well-worn path of daily obligations and this becomes our habit. It actually does become our habit—we have established neural pathways that have formed our beliefs and thinking because we keep repeating the same processes and we don't even have a thought or a choice about an activity anymore, we just do it automatically because that's what we do! We know that the pathways that stop being used, shrivel up, a bit like a disused road that becomes covered in weeds, it's the well-trodden paths that stay open. That's not to say we can't create a new path, but it does take conscious effort!

Everything we do is a choice, often we're just not aware that we are making those choices.

If we shed awareness or light on our choices, perhaps some of the things we are doing that seem so mundane, like hanging out the washing, for example, can become more pleasurable and positive. We can think about *why* we do this, and instead of being the martyr, we can think about how this is helping everyone in our family, we can be grateful for the clothes we have to wash, be grateful for the beautiful sunshine to dry the clothes, be grateful for the opportunity to stand out in the fresh air while we hang out the washing and so on. We can be grateful for the people who made the clothes, who sold them in the shop, for the people who made our automatic washing machines, for the people who delivered systems to our houses so we can turn on a tap and have running water. Miracles are around us everywhere we look. So we can continue our "mundane" activities but our perspective can change.

On a more meaningful basis perhaps, is the question that tackles our purpose, what do we really want to be when we grow up? This is a hard answer to tease out of yourself when you are lost. I find the easiest way to make inroads to what you really want to be doing with your life is to consider the following question.

If you had all the time and the money in the world, what would you be doing?

What are your dreams? Can you remember them?

Perhaps, like me, you've always wanted to be an author. But to me that seemed to be something other people do, people who are gifted with language, people who are gifted with insight that others don't possess, people with a message that other people want to hear. You may have a dream but you may not feel that you fit into it. Consider what is it that is stopping you from doing what you really want to do?

I would encourage you to contemplate this, to try to remember what your passion was, if you don't feel you have a passion now. What would fill your cup? What do you enjoy doing most?

This exercise that follows is a pretty simple one that I first heard about from Alan Cohen, author of A Course in Miracles Made Easy. Essentially the breakdown is that there are really only two basic/primal emotions that we experience—love and fear—and all our other emotions stem from those. This is probably not new information to you, many teachers and authors discuss this concept and the fact it comes from so many different sources, makes it more likely to be so in my opinion. It is a simple but profound way to analyse how we are feeling, why we are doing what we are doing, and also, why we are not doing what we want to be doing! It is not possible to be operating from both states at once, yes we can fluctuate between the two, but we can't possibly be feeling fear and love at the same time, one state will always be dominating the other.

Alan's suggestion is to think about something that is troubling you (I thought about why I don't finish writing my book!), and think about what "fear" is telling you about it.

Some of the thoughts generated by fear for me were:

- Why would anyone want to listen to what you have to say?
- You're not really a writer, you're not good enough.
- You're a physiotherapist, how can you be writing about grief, you're not a psychologist.
- Your story isn't unique.
- You're not a creative writer.
- What will other people think of you?
- And the list went on ...

When you continue to listen to those thoughts in your head, it's no wonder you become discouraged.

I then sat and contemplated what love says to me about writing my book and these thoughts came to mind:

- Everyone has a story to tell.
- If you can help one person, it's worth it.
- You have had great feedback on courses you have run already.
- You can write in your own way.
- You care about others.
- You are worthy.

So the challenge then becomes to focus on love rather than fear. The emotions and feelings generated by love include – joy, peace, contentment, compassion, gratitude, connection, happiness, ease ... which equate to a physically relaxed state. Some of the emotions and feelings generated by fear include – jealousy, derision, anger, frustration, depression, separation, dis-ease, discontent ... which equate to the physical sensations of discomfort, uneasiness, anxiety and more.

When we feel suffocated, restricted and unable to move then fear is the culprit. When we are in flow, when we are relaxed, confident and calm, we are operating from love. Fear grips onto us, so we become immobilized, love sets us free and we feel safe in our wanderings.

In order to reclaim your dreams and your passions, you need to make them big enough that they are worth putting effort in for, they become worth striving for. If they are mediocre, they won't sit at the forefront of your mind and you won't have the desire and persistence to achieve them. So don't be afraid to dream big! We should be afraid of not dreaming and staying small!

This journey to working out who we want to be and who we want to meet continues to evolve throughout our lives. I know I want to continue writing, I want to continue with meditation group work and I believe my purpose is helping others and there are many ways in which I can do this.

So please take the time to sit down and work out what you want to be, what thoughts are blocking you, or holding you back? If you are feeling stuck here, consider what you enjoy doing the most in your life, what part of your work do you really connect with or get satisfaction from? Try to narrow this down to the fundamental aspect of what it is you enjoy. For example, if you are a software engineer and you finish a project, what was the part of this that you enjoyed? Was it writing endless lines of code? Was it problem solving? Was it helping others achieve what they wanted through your process? Was it being able to listen and help people clarify exactly what they need? Was it being innovative and approaching the issue from a less obvious angle?

Gay Hendricks talks about uncovering our purpose by examining the things we love and why we love them by taking off the layers of the initial thought. He uses the example of Russian dolls and taking them out one by one until you have narrowed it down to what your area of genius or your special gift is.

We need to find out what our purpose is, what we feel our strengths and desires are. I believe our true desires are our purpose. Once we find our purpose, find our strengths, we are on the right track to becoming who we are destined to be. It doesn't mean we all need to become Bill Gates or Richard Branson or Kim Kardashian. The world needs *you* in your best form. We are all integral cogs in the wheels of life and existence. If you were not here, the world would be changed. I do believe you need to become your priority and in doing so and in being the best version of you that you can be, others will truly benefit from being connected with you.

We can keep it real and realise that yes, we can have financial obligations that require us to make some money to survive, so maybe we can't change what we're doing overnight. But is there some element of choice in how we spend our time when we're not working that could serve to help us to work towards who we want to be? Can we take a break from TV, social media and other mindless activities to create what we want to do? How many hours in a day are spent in purposeful pursuit of becoming our best selves?

We need to start to make attachments to things that are truly important to us, to help us become the best we can be. Having the best house, the best cars, and the most expensive shoes is really putting a lot of energy into inert objects that don't really give us anything back. Real happiness, joy and love come from within ourselves and from those we are surrounded by, not from our possessions. We can move house, we can change cars, we can buy new clothes and we may feel better for a little while. But how long will it be until we need to change things again? Once we feel connected to ourselves, we will know exactly what sort of life we would like to be living, where we would like to live and why. If you find you are someone who is always changing things, seeking pleasure from external sources such as material things, you may want to really consider why this is so. Perhaps you are seeking the approval of others. When you approve of yourself, you will care less about what others think of you (and where you live, what you drive, what you wear and so on …).

You know you have this one life to live right now; it's never to late to change how you're living it and make this life worthwhile. We can make plans and start to make changes.

I wonder how many people are like me, and after the loss of every person they have loved or had connection with, they have made a pact to honour that person's life by living their own to the fullest, and within a week or two, they've got stuck back in the rut of obligation and blah? Back on the well-trodden path of mundaneness—without your dreams, without a vision of what you really want in your life—you are truly aimless!

Workbook Activity

Try to start to determine your purpose. What (and who) would you love to be if money and time were not an issue for you? What is stopping you from doing that? What are the negative comments you hold about this? What are the comments that would come to you from love about doing that? Keep this information for Chapter 8 where you will investigate your purpose in more depth.

Now, thinking back to the last chapter and thinking about *how* you want to be (rather than *what* you want to be):

Where would you like to be on the following scales—the same activity as the last chapter but now we are looking at what our ideal position would be on the scale. Which ones can you start to work on first?

In the comments section, try and work out what is stopping you from changing your behaviour? Is it love or fear-based? What are you afraid of?

Motivation

Procrastination

Direction

Love

Connectedness

How can you restore motivation? You may be able to find some blockers to your motivation and these may also be contributing to your overall procrastination. Addictive behaviours can be very disruptive in keeping your life on track and your mind body and soul in balance. For me, it signals I am seeking happiness from something outside of myself, that I am not enough to create my own happiness. Common addictive behaviours include excessive alcohol use, smoking, unhealthy eating, non-prescription drug use, prescription drug use, gambling, excessive social media interaction and more. Are you able to identify any behaviour(s) that may be influencing your motivation and procrastination? List these in your workbook.

Alcohol use crept into my life from occasional social drinking to drinking every night. I would see alcohol as my "reward" for a busy day at work, and as we stopped going out so frequently, I would drink at home. I never drank during the day but knew that drinking alcohol stopped me from completing many of the unfinished tasks I had piling up around me. I had a whole year alcohol free and found I did still enjoy myself at social functions and felt great. But once my goal of "one year alcohol free" had been reached, I slipped back into my old ways. I have been contemplating this issue and now, I make a conscious decision about whether I choose to have a glass of wine and why I want one. I feel more in control of my life and my purpose, am sleeping better and am healthier for it. Surrounding yourself with like-minded people and also talking about your issues, while it might be painful to do so at the time, helps you to heal. The problem with some of these behaviours is that our society promotes them as social, healthy activities. In Australia, alcohol is promoted widely through tourist and lifestyle ads, is associated with sporting activities and is seen as an acceptable way to wind down. It's what happy social people do! But in my experience, it's what unproductive people do!

A participant from one of my *From Grief to Gratitude* workshops described how she was constantly eating unhealthy food, despite knowing it was not the right choice for her. Another participant reported exercising excessively, to the point of being completely run down and suffering multiple injuries and illnesses. Many participants report excessive use of alcohol—this is common in Australia, I guess because it's legal most think it must be okay for your health! A conversation I had with a medical specialist (who has sadly since passed away), was very enlightening—the number of people who are ill and dying from irreversible liver failure from alcohol is huge in Australia, according to The Australian Institute of Health and Welfare, in 2010-2012 liver disease was the 11th leading cause of premature death in Australia (food for thought).

Other participants report increasing social isolation and withdrawal as a major influence on motivation and procrastination. Some of the *From Grief to Gratitude* participants report a lack of socializing with friends—not having them over as often, not going to friends' houses, not holding dinner parties or attending events held by friends. Watching TV, excessive social media interaction, lack of community engagement, cancelling on events, comfort eating, excessive busyness, excessive exercise, reading, staying late at work, obligating themselves to others were commonly raised too. Others report a lack of actually attending, engaging or participating in others' activities because they are not sure how they are going to handle their emotions in front of other people. Some just simply could not be bothered with dealing with anything "outside" their ordinary!

So where does grief fit in with love and fear? Initially, I think grief is borne from love. If we didn't love something, if we weren't attached to it, we wouldn't experience grief when we no longer have it. With chronic grief, I think fear creeps in, and we become fearful of living without what we have lost, we fear if we let go of our grief then we will forget what we loved. In reality, I believe if we let go, we truly let go, we are free to express our love, to find gratitude in having had the opportunity to love what we have lost and find the desire to carry on and experience more love in our life. If we hang onto grief, we sink into despair, depression, anger, frustration, misery, resentment—all emotions that are manifested by fear.

So it's a circle and it's a choice! We can make that choice actively, on purpose by refusing to stay in fear and choosing love. That way we can move forward.

Here are some emotions and states of mind I have listed under fear and love, perhaps you can think of others to add, feel free to pop them in right here—feel free to write in your book!

Fear
Unsettled
Anger
Resentment
Bitterness
Frustration
Depression
Apathy
Disappointment
Unhappiness
Judgemental
Confused
Anxious
Grief – chronic

Love
Settled
Happiness
Joy
Contentment
Peace
Passion
Grief (early)

Connection
Compassion
Sympathy
Gratitude
Happiness

Which emotions do you want to feel more of? Can you choose to focus on thoughts that come from love? If you can choose more loving thoughts, then surely it follows that you can begin to feel these emotions again. Generally if you are feeling settled you are feeling love, if you are feeling unsettled you are coming from a state of fear. Our physical health follows the state of our emotional well being, so when we are settled we are generally well, when we are unsettled we are often unwell.

We can choose to change our mind and hence choose our emotional state, by simply taking it back to a state of love rather than a state of fear. I used to think this was easier said than done, in actual fact the choice of state is easy, it's just that sometimes we don't want to change. Maybe we're just not used to being happy!

Gay Hendricks refers to our tolerance for happiness in his book, The Big Leap. He believes we have evolved to only stay in a state of happiness for a predetermined length of time, once we realize we are feeling really happy, we start to think about something negative to take this away from us. This may be so, but we can choose to focus our awareness to acknowledge that this is happening and actively change our mind back to a more peaceful state. It really is just about being aware and mindful of our state and using our ability to make a choice!

What we feel, influences the hormones circulating through our bodies—when we are stressed, we have more cortisol and adrenaline and norepinephrine circulating through us, when we are happy, the levels of happy hormones such as serotonin, oxytocin, endorphins, dopamine, melatonin, GABA are increased. Bruce Lipton (author of *The Biology of Belief*) describes how the emotional state influences our physiology at a cellular level. He has placed cells in petri dishes with the happy hormones and the cells continue to grow very well. When the cells are placed in a solution containing the stress hormones, they stop growing. Bruce Lipton began this research in the early 1970's and was regarded as a bit of a nutty professor at this time. Between 1987 and 1992, his research at Stanford University's School of Medicine revealed that the environment our cells are in, operating through the membrane, controlled the behaviour and physiology of the cell, turning genes on and off. This field of study is now referred to as epigenetics. This was radical information because up until this time, it was thought that environment did not control cellular activity, the genes did. Further research has come from this showing the connection between mind and body. Our state of mind, influences our body at a cellular level!

This is pretty mind-blowing stuff for me. So, not only do we have the ability to change our mind to change how we feel emotionally, we know that changing how we feel can change our physical state and wellbeing! It adds further weight to the argument that we have the ability to heal ourselves through meditation. Ian Gawler's book "The Mind that Changes Everything" discusses how to do this in a practical way.

Changing the way we feel can be a matter of perception; it can also be based on our existing belief systems (conditioning) and what has been modelled to us in the past. For example, when I encountered a baby brown snake (an extremely venomous snake) in my home office, I was terrified. The adrenalin was running through my body as I sat frozen, waiting to see what was going to happen. The snake was between the open door and me. It seemed to stop, look at me, turn around and slither on out the door, hiding under the cubby house! If I was used to having snakes in my environment as pets, or if I was a veterinarian with a special interest in reptiles, my response would have been quite different. Perhaps this would have been a joyful experience, feeling blessed at coming so close to the snake. My terror was based on my fear of snakes, which was passed on to me by my parents—my mother who is similarly terrified and my father who explained how dangerous these venomous snakes are and are to be avoided at all costs. In reality, I should be less scared of them now as my two similar experiences of snakes are that they have just left me alone. (I'm still working on that!). My state of fear was a temporary one (despite being heightened further by a huntsman spider dropping on my hand as I closed the blind in the office before making my dash across the backyard to the safety of the house!). It was a fight or flight response and necessary for my survival. However, when we stay in a state of stress or fear, we can develop chronic health issues such as hypertension, cardiac disease, high cholesterol and more. Can you see how unhelpful it is to stay in a state of fear rather than a state of love? Practicing the shift between the two is important in changing your life back to gratitude (and back to health).

Unless you are a spiritual master, it will be quite normal to fluctuate between states of fear and love, but the important lesson here is to develop awareness, so you can assess how you are feeling and why you are feeling this way. Keep it simple, is it fear or love? Can you change it? Do you want to change it?

Workbook Activity

1. Start by identifying behaviours that may be influencing your motivation and procrastination – we discussed some of these earlier in the chapter.
2. Just note some of your repeated behaviours and identify whether you are acting out of fear or love when you are behaving that way.
3. Summarise who you want to be (and remember this can continue to change throughout your life, it doesn't have to be your forever end point).
4. Start with writing some affirmations, which form part of the imagery that you can use to achieve your goals.

Write it down now: I will use me as an example. It's best to express your affirmations in the present – as if you are that now – because if that is your purpose, you already are – you just don't know it yet!

I, Marion Turner, am a writer.

Keep it present tense, the mind responds to what's happening now, and it responds to belief. So if you don't feel you believe this but you want to, perhaps you can write:

I, Marion Turner, am open to believing I am a writer.

Many of us have needed the approval of others to achieve our goals. So with this in mind, it can be useful to write our affirmations in the first, second and third person, so you are not hearing it only from yourself, but as if others are saying it to you and about you. This can solidify the thought in your head and give it more weight. I learned this extension of affirmations through the Soul Pleaser course with Tracy Secombe and find it adds strength to affirmations, as well as creating some fun when you are saying them to yourself.

It goes like this:

I, Marion Turner, am a writer
You, Marion Turner, are a writer
She, Marion Turner, is a writer

Saying these out loud in the mirror, looking yourself in the eyes as you say it is a powerful experience. I have been known to do this while driving the car (solo of course) and it is an uplifting experience. Say it often enough and it materialises – please try it, what do you have to lose?

Start with whatever resonates with you most – it may be about confidence, finding joy, being healthy, having fun, socializing – whatever you feel strongly about.

Chapter 4

Finding You - Love What You Do, Do What You Love

"Let the beauty of what you love be what you do."
Rumi

Joy matters. So all the little things that bring us joy matter – whether it's en"joy"ing cupcake, a dinner with friends, your son's soccer goal, all the things that bring us joy, matter. The key to joy is practicing gratitude and gratitude can be practiced through mindfulness. We can experience and express our gratitude in different ways; we just need to shift our focus to acknowledge what we have to be grateful for. We don't need to rank levels of joy or gratitude; joy is joy, it's just that, it is what makes us feel alive. When we can feel our own joy, we can recognise the pain we have had in grief. We need contrasts in our lives so we can see where we're at in any point in time. If we never experienced happiness, we wouldn't be aware that we were unhappy—the ups and downs of life and emotions are normal and necessary. So when we can recognise the pain in our grief, we have the opportunity to choose to opt out of the grief; we don't have to deny joy in our lives. In the same vein, having joy doesn't mean we are denying pain exists, we are just choosing to inhabit one state more than the other. The magnitude of your grief doesn't mean you loved someone more than someone else did, it's just the way yours is, but do we need to stay there? I don't think so.

So what do we have to be grateful for? How can we feel gratitude when we feel pain?

It's in the little things, like sitting outside in the sunshine when the forecast is for rain—which is what I am doing right now, it feels like 20 degrees (which is warm for July in South Australia), there is a gentle breeze blowing and beautiful blue skies, dappled with clouds. Sure, it's going to change to rain, everything changes but why not appreciate every moment for what it really is. I'll enjoy the rain when that comes too because I love weather. I've heard people say, "If we didn't have weather we wouldn't have something to complain about!" Well, I'm sure we would find something else to complain about, and yes of course, I've complained many times about the searing 42-degree heat and the freezing wind that chills me to my bones. But pretty much most of the time, I really like the weather. I was actually very keen for it to rain as soon as possible, I had brought the washing in, fertilised the lawn, got what I needed to do before the rain and I started to become a little impatient. Staying one step ahead of the weather is like a game to me! I like to get the washing in just before it rains, I like to wash my car and it not get rained on for a few days - you know the stories - I'm sure you have your own. But as I stood outside eagerly awaiting the rain clouds, I saw the beauty in what was here now and so I'm soaking it up. I've set my office up outside—feeling gratitude for the external power point we had installed, my beautiful secondhand teak outdoor setting, my wind chimes gifted to me years ago by my brother-in-law and sister-in-law, the company of my six month old puppy, who is content to lie on a rug on the concrete, next to my feet while I'm out here, instead of trashing the back lawn with the exciting new scent of fertiliser. All is good. And I'm sure, if you look for it, a lot of things are good in *your* life right now. We just have to stop and think about it. That's what mindfulness is about—it's about being present RIGHT NOW, not thinking about before or later, but NOW! Feeling the moment through all your senses and accepting it for what it is, not judging, simply observing. You don't need a monumentous occasion to feel joy—it's in the little things too!

Back to writing my book; here's the thing, it's really difficult to get your head around writing a book, when you don't feel you have a handle on everything—when you're not perfect. It's taken me a long time to realise that perfection will likely never come so it's time to just get on with it now. Because there are thousands of other people around the world who are at the same stage as you and I are now. That's the way it works. There are people at the front (whatever and wherever that is), people at the back (again, wherever that is) and people strewn throughout the space between. So like me, now is the time for you to get on with whatever it is you should be doing instead of waiting for it to be the right time or for you to have all the knowledge you need.

Obviously, you don't start operating on people until you've finished medical school and surgical training but you get what I mean. If it's something that involves you putting your head down, bum up and getting on with your life in a positive way, then just do it. Who knows where your eventual resting place will be, when you will have reached the point where you are not going to learn anymore. We have to let go of the fear of failure or the fear of not being good enough and just give what we have to give right now. It reminds me of the thought I used to have as a child when I was being driven in a car – we used to look out of the windows back then for entertainment (we didn't have electronic devices back then and reading in the car was not always a pleasant experience)! When there were no cars visible in front of us, I used to wonder if we were in the front of everyone, like we were the leaders. And I used to feel a slight disappointment when a car would appear up ahead as we rounded a corner – but it was a mixed feeling: a feeling of disappointment but also a feeling of connection that we had other people out on the road with us, and when someone passed us travelling in the opposite direction, that there was never just one way to go. I still think about that analogy and I think it's applicable to our whole lives, we are not alone on our journeys, there is always someone ahead, someone behind and there are many different ways to our destination, our journeys are not the same but we are all on one, whether we recognise it or not.

And if we think we're alone in grief, it just isn't true. According to the Ecology Global Network, in 2011, it was estimated that 55.3 million people die each year, 151,600 die each day and 6,316 people die each hour. It wouldn't be unrealistic to imagine 10 people being affected by each death, raising these figures by an order of magnitude for the people affected by grief caused by death around the world. And that doesn't include those suffering grief through loss of health, loss of relationships, loss of jobs, loss of homes and loss of communities and anything else of importance to the individual. So I think it's safe to say you're not alone. We are not alone. We can feel very alone when we isolate ourselves through withdrawing from social activities, by not talking to others about our problems, but it doesn't have to be that way. You only have to watch the news to see examples of grief every day – natural disasters, murders, robberies, house fires …

Our practice of over-working, of becoming so busy we don't have time to think, busy doing things for other people, leads us to becoming not only disconnected with everyone else, but with ourselves. We forget what we used to love to do, what fired us up to get out of bed in the morning, what things brought use real joy, what we felt our purpose was. We just jump on the treadmill of life and forget to live; we just mindlessly put one foot in front of the other until the day is done, go to bed and get up the next morning to do the same. Sound familiar? We forget what it's like to look forward to something, to plan, to dream, did you have trouble remembering what your dreams were in the previous chapters? Are you too scared to plan or dream now in case it doesn't come true? One things for sure, if you don't plan or dream, that's the sure way to make sure nothing happens! What do we find ourselves thinking about when we're trudging through the treacle? Are we even thinking about what we're doing, or are we ruminating? Are we going over negative thoughts in our head, imagining negative outcomes before they've happened, are we anxious about putting ourselves out there? Are we feeling hard done by with nothing left in our lives to feel grateful for? Well, we can choose to stay feeling that way. Just as we can choose to feel like that, we can choose to change our minds to act differently. Sounds too good to be true? It's not. It's about changing your perspective and practicing gratitude – not just saying thank you but really feeling the gratitude with all of your senses.

We need to come to our senses if we want to change our mind. We need to start experiencing our lives in a real felt sense, not mindlessly existing.

So how do we do that? First and foremost, we need to find elements of joy in our every day life.

We need to stop making up stories about what's happening and work with truth, or what just is—that is the truth, rather than what we THINK the truth is. You have most likely heard about real and apparent truths—and we often jump to the worst conclusions in our apparent truths. For example, you send a message to someone on Messenger explaining why you can't commit to what they would like to do, imagine it's a dinner invitation. When they don't reply immediately or worse, for a day or two (and you can see they've read the message), you have now decreed the reason for them not answering. They're annoyed with you, or not interested in catching up with you, now that you've decided not to go along with what they want. Worse still, they probably don't like you anymore, and are telling everyone else that you've pulled out at the last minute and let them down. Now everyone knows and they're probably all talking about you by now! Sound familiar?

What a load of crap you've just made up in your head! What are the possible alternative scenarios here? Well, they are limitless but here are some possibilities I've come up with:

- They actually replied and forgot to hit send (have done that myself many times!).

- They got halfway through replying and got distracted by a phone call and forgot to finish the message.
- Their phone went flat.
- They lost their phone.
- They read your message, were thinking about replying when they started to feel violently ill, or had a heart attack!

Who knows? They do and you don't! It's that simple really. Fabricating this nonsense in your mind is creating your own anxiety. Worry is really just excessive thinking and it's important to learn and practice letting things go. You'll find out the response when you're supposed to, and if you're unable to let go, why not write another message and ask if they're okay? We often take these situations as a personal attack, but we have made that up in our minds, can you think of times when you have done that yourself? I have had instances of clients not returning for treatment after I have seen them once and assumed I didn't help them, or they didn't like my treatment only to find when they return a year later, that they were fixed in one session and very happy! It's a big lesson in how we can create drama and anxiety in our life, I could just as easily have thought they were better—that is my preferred option now, I will become concerned or worried when I have to, not just because I can!

We think worry grips us, but we choose to hang onto it. We can choose to drop it in an instant but we're just not used to doing that. Adopting different ways to handle your thoughts and taking a step back and changing your perspective can be very powerful.

And while we're on thinking about other people, how well do you *listen* when other people are talking? Are you actually engaging in the conversation and really listening or are you waiting for them to finish so you can say what you need to say? This happens a lot in argumentative or confrontational situations in particular, where people aren't really taking into account the other person's point of view, they're just keen on being heard themselves. It's useful to practice active listening and you can start that right now. When someone else is talking, really listen to what they're saying and avoid the temptation to interrupt them. How can you have a response to what they're saying when you haven't listened to them or let them finish saying it? Do you have special telepathic powers that negate the need for others to verbally communicate with you? Probably not. And I'm betting you find it annoying when others interrupt you when you are talking too. This is quite a difficult habit to break and one that requires practice. But really, it just requires you to be present in the moment and to listen. And then speak your truth back. If this is an issue with your partner in particular, do try this and when the same respect is not afforded to you, perhaps stop talking or gently point out that you have been trying to actively listen to them without interrupting and perhaps they might like to try it too. I have found this to be particularly powerful when talking to my children, especially when someone else is trying to ask you something while you're engaged in a conversation. Point out that you are listening to someone right now and you will be attend to them in due course and they will also have your full attention when it's their turn. Encourage others to ignore their electronic devices when having a conversation and of course, lead by example with that.

This year, I have experienced both ends of the spectrum with people's listening practices. On the first occasion when both my husband and I were being interrupted and talked over in a meeting we attended together, I didn't really have the clarity of mind at the time to point out that we weren't being heard. Instead, I clammed up and let the other person talk. My husband talked to this person on another occasion by telephone and it became a conversation where he was being talked over, so he continued to talk anyway, while the other person interrupted. Even so, this will not have resulted in effective communication from either side. On the flipside of this, I was talking to a teacher about an issue at school with my son, and I was so taken aback by his ability to listen and communicate that I later thanked him in an email and told him he will be my "poster boy" for communication in my mindfulness courses. What a treat it was to be listened to respectfully, for him to consider his response after I finished talking, and to make sure he understood what I was saying. Another joy of the contrasts in our world, if we didn't have the underwhelming side, we wouldn't appreciate the brilliant side!

Sometimes, if you have something really important to say and you fear you will not be heard, write it down instead! Writing gives you clarity and space to say what you really want to say and if you don't judge yourself as you are writing, the truth will flow on out. You can then choose whether or not to send that to someone, or rehearse a conversation.

When you experience a feeling of unease with communication with someone, whether it is electronically or in person, take the time to try to see the issue from different points of view and imagine the possibilities within the situation. You may not always jump to the right conclusion; it is entirely possible that you are jumping to a conclusion based on your current belief system, some of which is based on experience, some of which is based on assumption. Changing the way we respond to people is really about adopting different perspectives, thinking more deeply about where the other person is coming from and giving that adequate consideration.

In philosophical terms, perspective is basically a point of view, an attitude of how someone thinks about or sees a situation. Perspective is malleable and we can use this to our advantage in our daily lives too. Our lives are filled with many repetitive activities—that we often view very negatively, they become chores—onerous tasks. Chores are defined as necessary but tedious tasks. But they are there day in day out, and we generally have to do them if we want some order in our lives. Who determines if they are tedious? We do. We have discussed this a little earlier regarding washing clothes!

I first came across this next workbook activity in a Mindfulness-Based Stress Reduction course (based on the teachings of Jon Kabat-Zinn) run by a wonderful meditation teacher and fellow physiotherapist Georgie Davidson. She was my introduction to mindfulness meditation and I have been grateful for her ever since! This was the beginning of my road to becoming a meditation teacher.

Please don't skip forward here, do this activity; it's an important one.

Workbook Activity

Take out your workbook and jot down your typical daily routine in a list format.

Now, next to each activity, assign an N or a D (or B for both if you feel it's appropriate) to each activity. N stands for nourishing and D stands for draining. A nourishing activity is one that lifts your energy levels and you find enjoyable, in fact you generally stay present during these activities whereas a draining activity depletes your energy levels. The draining activities generally pull you down and can make you feel tense or aggravated, waiting for them to be over or you take the opportunity to extend the misery by thinking about all the things in your life that are unfair, so you can make the most of your miserable plight! Or you may put the draining ones off because you don't have the energy to tackle them. You are basically assigning your judgement on each activity here, and sometimes it may be both.

Now, is your day overwhelmingly nourishing or draining? Or is it a mix of both? Do you find some activities are sometimes draining and on other days are nourishing depending on how you feel?

We don't need to do much work on the activities that are nourishing, and in fact, they should be keepers. What about the draining ones? If they are necessary but boring or draining, what are you usually thinking while you're doing them? Are you being a martyr e.g. " Why am I the only one who ever cleans the toilet in this house?"— are you really focusing on the activity or are you thinking about what else you would rather be doing, that you are being denied the opportunity to do because you are stuck with this task? Are you able to turn your head around and change your perspective with these activities? What about the feeling of gratitude for having toilets, dishes, so many clothes that you need to do washing every day? If you immerse yourself in the activity – e.g. washing dishes, how does the warm water feel on your hands? How does the dishwashing detergent smell? What about the squeaky sensation when the grease has dissolved, and how nice and sparkly the dishes look once they're washed?

Find one activity on your "draining" list and have a go, see if you can turn it around. This is a simple but profound practical experience of how much control you actually have over your feelings, *you can change your mind* and that's a powerful thing! Being present and mindful opens your eyes to everyday experiences and thoughts which can be very pleasant—we deny ourselves this experience when we begin ruminating and allow our bad moods to fester. You *can* overcome your habitual way of thinking and move forward and once you start with one activity, you can see how easy it is to apply this to others. Perhaps you used to enjoy doing some of the things that you now find draining? You can change that—give some of the things away or delegate them to someone else if you feel you're truly overwhelmed with some parts of your life, asking for help can be a lifesaver! If you're over doing the housework all by yourself, get others within the home to help you, or find a way to get a cleaner. Alternatively, change your perspective towards the activity. Maybe you're cleaning the house because it makes you feel better when the house is clean, rather than you're cleaning the house because no-one else can be bothered. Can you see the difference?

You can also add to this list, perhaps write a list of things you would like to include in your day if you had the time/money/ motivation etc. things you used to find nourishing. Mark them with a massive N!

Mindfulness Activity

Find one activity each day to engage yourself in mindfully. Perhaps it's taking a mindful shower, feeling the sensation of the water on your body, the smell of the shampoo and body wash, the temperature of the water, the sound of the water running onto the floor …

It's often these repetitive activities that we gloss over that can actually be enjoyable – we are going to do them anyway, so why not experience it? Spend your time in joy and appreciation and gratitude instead of burdening yourself with stress!

Go for a mindful walk – notice the shadows on the ground, the movement of the leaves and the branches in the breeze, the sky, the clouds, the birds, the colours, the feeling underfoot as you tread lightly on the ground. Slow it down, take it in; learn to nourish yourself.

Chapter 5

Resistance

"Yesterday I was clever, so I wanted to change the world.
Today I am wise, so I am changing myself."
Rumi

I often wonder what it is that stops us from doing the things that we know are good for us. For example, knowing we should exercise daily, to not eat junk food, to take some time out for ourselves. I find it interesting and it raises its head daily for me at work as a physiotherapist—not just for myself but also in my clients. Let me give you an example. Brenda comes for treatment of her ongoing hip pain which has caused her grief for a number of years, she has had three cortisone injections for her bursitis at the hip, has seen the occasional physiotherapist but things aren't changing. On examination, I can see that she's tight in various muscle groups, lacks the ability to activate particular muscles when standing on one leg and I explain that this is likely to be a contributing factor to her ongoing issue. I go on to treat her and explain that I can give her the tools to correct this muscle imbalance but it will require her to do some exercises and stretches which will help create a new neural pathway (or restore the original one) that will help her to maintain her hip in the long term. She seems concerned that I've identified a problem, I'm actually happy I have—we have something we can work with and it's something that I've seen resolve many times in the past.

I review Brenda in one week's time and ask how the exercises are going. Guess what? She hasn't been doing them! I even have the capacity to send her the exercises via a mobile phone app and she can follow the video instructions if she has forgotten them after I've shown her and she's still not doing them. When I ask why she hasn't done them she replies she's been too busy! Too busy to fit in 5-10 minutes worth of exercises daily to help solve a problem that has been bothering her for years!

I see two issues here. Firstly, people are often looking for a quick solution—the cortisone injection, some tablets, some trigger point dry needling and then they can move on with their routine—they don't want to put in effort to change anything to make things better. This is the second issue I see; a lot of people don't want to take ownership of their situation. She's also not interested in losing some weight, which might also help the situation because she "has tried everything in the past and nothing ever works for her". I used to take these situations personally, that I was unable to help some people or I was inadequate at advising them to do their exercises. I have turned this around for myself now and I think it seems to be making a difference in the clinic too. I tell people they have actually paid me for my advice, they have given up time in their day to come for treatment (time they apparently don't have to do exercises) and I say, I can give you this information, but what you CHOOSE to do with it, is up to YOU!

With persistence you can overcome resistance!

It's the same with the exercises that follow in this book. I know I also have resistance to change in many areas of my own life, and certainly feeling my feelings was a major one of those! Resistance rears its head pretty much every time someone suggests something that challenges your current way of thinking. Acknowledging that resistance exists, is the first step to dropping it. We may not know the exact cause of the resistance but I think we can move past that without knowing it. Having to know the direct cause of the resistance, is just another issue that will hold you up, stop you moving on until you have the complete answer to everything in your life.

It's a bit like watching a slow flowing drain. You may be standing in the shower, noticing the water is starting to build up around your feet more than normal. You look to see why the water is not draining – there could be several reasons for this—maybe the drain is blocked by a bar of soap, maybe there is too much hair caught up in the trap—maybe it's blocked much more deeply and you can't see where or what the blockage is. Try removing the bar of soap or the clump of hair and watch the water flow down the drain. We often stand in the way of our own change like that bar of soap or clump of hair and once we acknowledge that, we can get out of our own way and move forward. Sometimes when the blockage is something we can't see, we may need to call in a plumber to help clear the drain. Sometimes we need to accept some help for ourselves from outside too. But this outside help is really clearing us out on the inside. I can definitely liken my resistance to my feelings like a deep inner block in my spiritual plumbing. Once I chose to accept that I was blocked, I then chose to let go, to stop the struggle and everything started to flow through me again. Sometimes I feel the energy flow through me like a rush, sometimes it's a trickle and the roots might be starting to invade again. But I can direct my light through these areas during meditation and clear them out. It's like my own drain cleaner root cutter! Maybe you can have a vision of something that works for you, that allows your energy to flow, that gets you out of your way.

Maybe your resistance is like a rock in the middle of a stream, that you can simply pick up and move out the way. Thinking of this now brings back a funny memory I have of Mostyn. We had a period of a few years where we used to play Putt-Putt (mini golf) whenever we got together. So we played in Victoria, New South Wales, Queensland – we had a championship going on – he was so competitive! Once, after an unusual result of him losing to both my husband and me, he snatched the score-card and tried to burn it with his lighter. Needless to say, we rescued the card; I even made him a t-shirt with this scorecard printed on it. I digress! I think the last time we played was in my hometown in Adelaide and the course was not a very professional one. It was a very hot day—around 38 degrees Celsius and we were struggling through the course. We identified difficult areas of the course for Moz and put him off by drawing his attention to the obstacle—and focused his attention on that (clay mushrooms in this case) and no matter how he tried, he couldn't get past them. On the next hole, Mostyn played off first and his ball made it through a tunnel in a hill and then came out the other side, landing near the hole. Both Ian and I were unable to get through the hill, our balls kept returning to us. The reason became apparent when we went around the back of the little hill to see what was going on, and Mostyn was laughing.

He had blocked the exit with a rock! Sometimes it's not only us applying the brakes. Others could be involved! We need to seek it out and remove it!

So resistance really stops us from moving forward. Sometimes it stops our awareness but I believe we are often cognizant of why we need to do things, but just don't know why we're not doing it. I believe we are not really willing to let go of the resistance, for whatever reason.

Maybe we are afraid of feeling our feelings properly because we know it's going to hurt. Maybe we're not really sure of how things are going to turn out if we change what we're doing. I really want you to think about this and really stop and think when you encounter resistance and see if you can try to let it go. When I encounter resistance to doing something that I know is really good for me, I just do it anyway—even though I don't feel like doing it—meditation for example. Without exception I feel better after and although it might have been a little distracted compared to other times, I am pleased with having done it.

Resistance presents itself as a flag for further investigation. Stop and ask yourself why, and then ask yourself if that is reasonable. Just last week I had an experience with my son being resistant to nearly every suggestion I had (not unusual for a 15 year old) and over the ensuing day I just felt exhausted, drained and felt I could not cope with my caseload at work for that day. I did something I haven't done for years. I rang the office, explained I was unwell and wouldn't be in until 4 o'clock and asked for the other appointments be re-scheduled. I took the time to sit with how I was feeling, I meditated, I allowed thoughts to come and go, I reflected, and I really sat and felt my feelings.

By 4 o'clock I was at work and I worked really productively for the rest of my session until around 9.30 that evening. I had so much more to give because I had given myself the opportunity to care for myself, loving myself and practice self-compassion! I dropped my resistance to self-compassion, I forgave myself (and my son) for how I was feeling and I felt renewed. I was on the edge of a meltdown that day, and my ability to recognise my issues with resistance to self-compassion seriously turned my day around. I was feeling physically ill that day too, and by 4 o'clock that afternoon, I was energised! I have learned so much from that experience. One was that I was really picking up on my son's resistance initially and I believe it highlighted the resistance I was feeling towards being compassionate towards myself.

You know, what we really have to learn is that all our feelings come and go, they constantly change and we don't really get to pick and choose which ones we will feel unless we take the opportunity to consciously change them. Feelings are going to be with us our whole lives. We need to feel them *all*, we need to get comfortable with what they are, what they mean to us and just accept them. I think most people would say they are reluctant to experience their feelings of sadness but when they do, when they truly experience them and have a good cry if that's what they feel they need to do, they feel much better after. We try to avoid the short-term discomfort but in reality, that just ensures we have issues for a much longer time, that is what turns situations into long-term problems. Allowing ourselves to experience, acknowledge and accept our feelings diminishes the power or the hold these emotions have over us. The resistance to feeling them stops our energy flowing through, we are clogging up our pipes! It's not the water that's the problem flowing through the pipes, it's the resistance in the pipes that's the issue – the roots, the hair, the bar of soap …

When we consider this, the beliefs we have are often what cause our resistance, it's our shame, our guilt, our sadness, our unworthiness, our unlovableness (yes, that is a word) that stop us moving forward. Our inability to forgive others, our need to blame, our lack of connection with all those around us, contribute to overgrowth of roots in the pipes. Remember, what we resist, persists (and gets bigger!)

And the wonderful thing is, we have the power to change this!

So when you experience parts of this *From Grief to Gratitude* process that you feel you want to skip over, or you just feel too tired to do – recognise this as resistance and just do it anyway.

Learn to let go – let go of the need to know everything, control everything, believe everything, be everything, blame others. Learn to let go of guilt, shame anger, and fear and you will come back to love.

Letting go of resistance, is really letting go of the struggle, of allowing a sense of ease back into your life. The resistance doesn't have to be there. We are just used to having it there, it doesn't mean it's good for us!

Workbook Activity

What are some things you do in your life that you know are not good for you?

What are some things you feel you could do in your life that would be good for you but you are not doing?

What are some of the reasons you are doing/not doing these things? Can you sit for a while and contemplate your resistance?

Meditation Practice

For this practice, I would like you to just sit quietly, perhaps settle yourself with a little mindfulness meditation to start with. Starting to relax, let go of the need to do anything else, space in front of your closed eyes, sounds inside and outside the room, follow the breath. Now spend some time contemplating how resistance looks for you, perhaps it's a boulder in a stream, roots in a pipe etc. and see yourself dissolving this block, this resistance. You may resolve it with light, with water, with an explosion, whatever works best for you but just sit with this and see where it takes you. Feel the feeling of letting go of the need for this resistance to be there.

Feel how much less painful it is to stop the struggle.

Chapter 6

Self-Compassion

"The worst loneliness is to not be comfortable with yourself."
Mark Twain

Do you feel things are starting to change for you now, are you starting to focus on some different aspects of your life? Can you start to see if you are coming from fear or love? Sometimes just asking yourself that question will shift your awareness to how you are behaving and reacting – this mindfulness leads to awareness and acceptance. You can be aware and may or may not be judgemental. If you are truly being mindful, you will be aware and non-judgmental—Jon Kabat-Zinn defines mindfulness as "non-judgmental awareness of the present moment".

Does self-compassion start with self-awareness or does self-awareness start with compassion? Acceptance of ourselves starts with awareness, so the work you have done so far has been important in uncovering who you are at the moment and now we need a willingness to look at ourselves and accept ourselves for who we are right now. Whether we are happy or satisfied with what we have uncovered is irrelevant right now, we need to be able to take a deep breath, acknowledge things for what they are and look upon this with a kind eye and accept who we are in this moment.

Once we can truly do that, we have the capacity for self-compassion. Just as we can look kindly upon a child who has a made a mistake because she didn't know better, we can look upon ourselves as someone who has become who they are with what they knew at the time. Just because we are "grown up" it doesn't mean we know everything! We don't always do everything right, we aren't perfect. We have our whole lives to learn, and personally, I feel I have started another huge learning curve in my 50's! It takes mistakes to foster growth, so I am grateful for the mistakes I have made along the way as they are teaching me how to become fulfilled now. Of course I didn't know this at the time, but now their purpose seems useful and it makes sense!

We need to start to give ourselves the compassion we readily give to others, I'm going to outline some issues that I have personally experienced which you may or may not relate to, but hopefully they bring up some thoughts in your own mind for issues you may be facing.

Chances are you don't feel worthy, deep down you don't think you are good enough and you don't love the way you are. For example, if you've put on weight and are neglecting how you eat or are neglecting to take regular exercise, perhaps that's a sign that you don't really love yourself enough to make the effort. It is such a common thing to feel unworthy of your own love, but you are likely to love others well. If you are feeding only yourself, do you put the same amount of effort in as you do when the whole family is eating together? Do you put the same effort in as you would if you had guests coming? Sit for a while and think about the motivation behind some of the things you do. Maybe you don't have time to exercise because you're busy doing things for other people. Well, wait a minute—you're worthy too!

I came to this realization about myself during the From People Pleaser to Soul Pleaser course with Tracy Secombe (who happens to be yet another physiotherapist – and also my cousin). I found this course invaluable because it really involved me thinking about myself and my behaviours and my willingness and need to please others before myself, much of which was based on old beliefs and conditioning. Tracy facilitated this course extremely well and has a gift for coaching others; I highly recommend this course. I re-read some of my course notes and in those I read a free flowing/writing exercise I did which was titled "What does Spirit/God think of me?" It's about a page long and reading it again now, brings tears to my eyes when I see how much I have moved forward and also how relevant the whole entry is to me. Two sentences stand out for me and I would like to share them with you, I hope you resonate with this too.

"Nothing will take away the feeling of loss but love.
Let yourself come back to you, you deserve this so
much and so do your family and friends."

This insight led me on to further exploration into self-compassion and to authors who have great insight into this, such as Kristen Neff and Rick Hanson among others.

We really need to lighten up on ourselves. We're not perfect, and nor is anyone else! We're no less perfect than others and for the majority of us, we are much more judgmental and harsh in our criticism of ourselves than we are of other people. We would never say the things to others that we repeatedly say in our heads to ourselves. Simple examples of the derision we show ourselves are what we say out loud or in our heads when we drop things "Stupid!" or "God you're hopeless!" Most of us would never dream of saying these things constantly to those around us, or to people we don't know! It probably comes as no surprise to you that we are often nicer to people we don't even know than we are to ourselves. Have a think about how you talk to yourself next time you make a mistake.

One of our biggest fears is that we are not good enough and we believe we are not worthy. As we peel away our layers, we inevitably find we have this judgement of ourselves because we don't love ourselves. We don't even know how to be kind to ourselves – which is a sad state of affairs when you think about that – you are the most important person in your own life, because without you, you wouldn't have a life and you wouldn't be able to care or love anyone else!

Do you love yourself?

Well, this came to me one day on reflecting why I didn't bother to exercise as I should, why I made poor food choices and why I didn't have personal goals or dreams anymore. My light bulb/aha moment for me was, I don't love myself! I didn't care enough about myself to make my life the best it could be! And why didn't I love myself? Because I didn't feel I was worthy enough! I had no idea of how I was going to get back to loving myself and finding self-compassion.

In the moments when we are truly enjoying ourselves, we are happy with everything – and that includes ourselves. It must mean that we have let go of the negativity we hold about ourselves for that moment in time, it has dissolved for a period of time, we have been able to look beyond those things and truly enjoyed an experience for what it was without feeling badly about ourselves. And if we have done that on at least one occasion, then we know it's possible! That's all we need to know.

So what makes us feel unworthy? Maybe it's comments from other people, maybe it's guilt or shame related to past behaviours or actions? Maybe we never truly felt valued by anyone? Maybe it's our harsh inner critic that expects us to rise above the human condition and be perfect at all times—I believe this was my major contributing factor, along with a sprinkling of everything else.

Just as we consider a mother's or father's love to be unconditional, or God's love to be unconditional, our love for ourselves needs to be unconditional also. True unconditional love does not require anything in return—it does not have conditions placed on it which is why it is UNconditional! There's no "I'll love myself when I've lost 10kg, or I'll love myself when I get a promotion ...

So I thought about why I didn't really love myself, and it turns out I have habits and thoughts that I would not particularly admire in someone else, I assumed I was the only person who thought like this—turns out I'm wrong—which is a great thing.

When I really think back to when I first had negative thoughts about myself, ironically, the major source of derision I remember is actually Mostyn—calling me fat, blubber, flatsy (a rubber doll that was flat—referring to my pre-pubescent chest state). I have a vivid memory of crying to my mum one night, sobbing that I was fat and Mum told me it was "puppy fat" and that it will go away. I am fortunate that this did not manifest into an eating disorder but I feel my feelings of unworthiness probably stemmed from this period of time. An earlier memory of my childhood was lying awake in bed one night when my parents had friends over from the football club. We had had a barbeque and my parents were enjoying some music and drinks – normal social activities and I had been sent to bed around 10 or 11 o'clock – which was not unreasonable considering my age. No other kids were at this barbeque apart from my brothers. I remember lying in my room (which was close to the lounge room in the first house we lived in) and hearing Dad say "Yes, she can be a bitch sometimes." I have thought of this from time to time and it still makes me feel uncomfortable. It doesn't upset me anymore as I'm a parent now and I understand that children can push your buttons and that was never said to hurt me. But I wonder if I have carried this through my life as well. In truth, I actually don't even know that this was even said about me – my memory of the preceding parts of the conversation is non-existent now, but I suspect there was reference to me in that for me to take it badly – but this could have been my first major "apparent truth" episode. I started to feel that I must have been an annoyance.

But the upside is, if you have stories like these, you can change them, some of the stories we have been told by others, along with stories that we have told ourselves are simply not true, or not that important. Stories are simply that – "a description of a true or imaginary event" (Cambridge English Dictionary). Whether you are the story-teller or someone else is, it is subject to perspective and interpretation! We can re-tell these stories to ourselves as well when we view it from a different perspective. My five-year-old self really took over-hearing my Dad to heart. My 53 year-old self understands that my Dad loves me, that he always has, that I used to talk a lot, that I probably was annoying at times – like most children can be – this comment would have meant nothing to him and if I asked him about it, he wouldn't remember it anyway, it would not have played a major role in his life, he would not have a story embedded in his memory about it. Unfortunately I can't really ask him about it now and get his most accurate recollection as he now has early Alzheimer's disease. Likewise with Mostyn calling me fat/blubber/flatsy. This was teasing from a sibling. Simple as that, yes, it's hurtful at times and no, I can't ask him about that either now but I'm convinced he would not have wanted this to affect me throughout my life. So it's time to forgive that, re-write the story and move on. Looking back at photos, yes, I was chubby in my pre-pubescent state, but when I look back on my mid to late teen years, even to pre 40 – when I thought I was fat all that time, I wish I looked like that now! Oh, to go back with the knowledge we have now. But we can all wish for that and it's really quite pointless. The core of the matter is, whatever the cause, perhaps there are reasons you don't love yourself or feel worthy.

The good news is, there is a way you can start to love yourself again. You can start right now, with loving who you are right at this moment. We can love ourselves no matter what state we are in. We can even love ourselves for not loving ourselves at the moment! No matter what predicament or situation we are in, we always have the ability to love ourselves. Just as we look upon our sleeping children with great love (even after a day of constant struggle), we can look upon ourselves with the same love and compassion. We need to really get to grips with the reality that we're not perfect, that we are allowed to make mistakes, and we always have now to make a difference. Starting with loving ourselves makes a massive difference. We need to become aware, acknowledge, accept and let go!

So really what I found through my grief was that I had undercurrents of other issues running through me that really came to the surface but I was blind to them. I just scooped everything up into the grief bucket and waited for it to disappear. But this wasn't working for me. While this has been an uncomfortable process, it has been cathartic because I can make the choice to let things go, to forgive where I need to and just get back to me!

I started by simply looking at myself in the mirror – but not just at myself (and I generally only had cursory glances at myself when getting ready – for reasons previously explained), but I spent time staring into my eyes in the mirror. Just looking - not expecting anything.

I started to tell myself I was worthy and open to being loved and loving myself. What a relief it was to allow this to flow. I started my affirmations in the car while driving alone, saying out loud something new each week. I Marion Turner am worthy of love. I, Marion Turner, love myself and that's great! As I mentioned previously, affirmations work well when done in the first, second and third person – so I did that too! "You Marion Turner, love yourself and that's great. "She, Marion Turner, loves herself and that's great."

When did you stop loving yourself? Was it through your loss? Did the pain of losing something pour concrete around your heart to stop you feeling love, so in the certainty of experiencing loss again, it won't hurt? I felt my heart was set in concrete. I discovered this during meditation, when I discovered I couldn't feel any physical sensation below the level of my heart in the feelings or centering meditation. I knew I was relatively devoid of feeling following Mostyn's passing (after the initial stage of grief and pain had passed) but it wasn't until a meditation insight that I saw the cracks appear around the covering of my grey heart and tiny glows of red emanating from the cracks until I felt such a burst of joy that my heart felt like it exploded, shattering the concrete and started beating again. This was such a powerful image for me and when I'm feeling numb, I now rekindle my heart through this imagery. You can use this too if you feel it resonates with you, perhaps you have an alternative image that comes to you.

And when you think of that image of concrete around the heart, it makes sense that not only can you not receive love when your heart is set in stone, you can't radiate it either! This concrete cast is not a one-way transmitter!

Do you have to know someone to be compassionate towards him or her? Definitely not – it is easy to feel compassion for someone you do not know at all – perhaps because you don't have any pre-existing judgement of them, you are able to just see their humanity and feel kindness and compassion towards them, even if they have done something terrible. Perhaps it's easier when you don't have full disclosure of all they have done or said in the past. Maybe this is why we find it hard to be compassionate towards ourselves, we know the truths, we know the details! As time passes though, the details can become sketchy, but we still hold onto the beliefs regardless.

It follows then that it is hard to feel compassion towards yourself because, you know yourself better than anyone else. You are the one who can hear the thoughts in your head, the judgement of others that you won't speak aloud, the jealousy, the misgivings, the shame, the guilt. It is hard to get out of your own way and feel compassion for yourself. It is hard to stop judging, speaking negatively, feeling the way you do. Even when you know things about other people, you are more ready to let them go, forgive and see reason. We need to spend time giving ourselves the same care. If we go back to the root emotions in our life of love and fear – shame, guilt, jealousy, judgement all stem from fear. You can choose to feel love and the emotions connected to that instead, you can choose to feel love for yourself no matter what!

So we can look at ourselves from the outside in with what's called a compassionate curiosity. It's a non-judgmental, kind look for more information that respects how we feel about what we find. For me it's like we're looking at things from two points of view – one as an external observer, the other as the internal source of the information. The external observer is not judging the source harshly, merely acknowledging and accepting what is, while the internal source feels no guilt or shame at offering up the information. The two points of view intersect at a point of mutual awareness.

Once we discover or uncover information, we can choose to acknowledge the existence of it. As Dr Phil would say, "We can't change what we don't acknowledge!" What do I mean by discover or uncover? When we discover something, we find something that was previously unknown, (we can also rediscover something that was previously known but forgotten again), but uncovering implies finding the existence of something that has been hidden. It's a funny game we play, but I feel some of what I have discovered about myself was more likely uncovered! I guess however it is brought to light is irrelevant; the important part becoming aware or awakening to ourselves. Once we can become aware, we can move on to acknowledgement, which is really just the acceptance of the existence of something. This is not complete acceptance however, to truly accept, you must let go of judgement and simply allow it to be so. When we have done so, we can choose to let go of any attachment to it.

It makes sense that we can't release something that we don't know exists. This is why it is so important to go through the exercises in the book and not avoid the ones we find difficult or painful. Don't let the resistance take over! It is important to sit with ourselves and remember. It is through the process of acknowledgement that we bring ourselves freedom through the ability to release our attachment to our beliefs. It's like we have been emancipated when we can finally do that. We can truly accept ourselves for who we are now, when we release the baggage, when we throw that suitcase as far away as we can with the zip open - so all the contents just fly away. I like to imagine this happening in a fierce windstorm so all the bits and pieces are caught up and blown away in a flurry and I could never chase after them and bring them back, even if I wanted to. Gone, let it go and breathe!

Just as you would give your best friend a hug if they were feeling down, or even just to say hello, it is nice to greet yourself in the same way. Making this a habit breaks down the barriers to self-compassion, as you start to see your self as part of the combined human spirit, of humanity, as part of our collective consciousness, and not as an isolated being. You can practice this by closing your eyes, following your breath and placing your hands on your heart. Feel the movement of the chest as you breathe, feel your hands gently touching each other, perhaps give one hand a reassuring squeeze or stroke as you breathe into your heart space, feeling the tension release – feel yourself giving yourself a hug, one of the long meaningful connecting hugs you give others. In your mind, tell yourself you care, tell yourself you love yourself, you are worthy, and let yourself be still. If your mind wanders (and it most likely will), return to the breath and the feeling of ease and comfort. See yourself as a child who needs your care and support. Feel what the sensation of feeling love feels like. They're called feelings because they're supposed to be felt!

So you may be wondering how self-compassion differs from self-indulgence and self-pity? Self-pity is generally unattractive and usually involves exaggeration or dramatization or catastrophising – "I never get the good things in life", I'll never have the house I want, Why me? …

Self indulgence on the other hand involves unnecessary and often unhelpful activities that are not beneficial to your whole life, for example, buying things you cannot afford, indulging in pleasures purely for yourself, often at the expense of others, doing exactly as you please without taking into consideration the needs/wishes of others. This is not to say you need to spend your life people-pleasing, of course you matter too, but *why* are you doing the things you are doing?

During one of the *From Grief to Gratitude* workshops, a participant related a question her psychologist had asked her; simple, profound and worth contemplating. "Do you do things *for* love or *in* love?" What is your motivation behind what you do for others? If you are doing things for love, perhaps this is a sign that you don't feel worthy, that you don't love yourself.

Self-compassion, is a mindful (non-judgmental) awareness of

your self that brings with it the ability to understand that you are not perfect, that you are allowed to make mistakes and this is common to all human beings, it also manifests as kindness to yourself. Kristin Neff has defined self-compassion as being composed of three main components: self-kindness, common humanity, and mindfulness. It involves being friendly, generous and caring towards yourself. Not something that we really practice in western society and we also look down on those who do care for themselves "She loves herself!" – Is that really such a bad thing?

We reward ourselves for pushing ourselves as hard as we can, to soldiering on when we're sick, for being strong and stoic and our ultimate reward for this behaviour is often sickness and depression! We reward ourselves for self-punishment! We don't allow ourselves the time to slow down, smell the roses and savour the moment. Of course we advise others to do this, but *we* don't need to because we're stronger than that and we can just push on! Well it's time to stop! It's time to take notice of how badly we are treating ourselves. When I visualise the way I have treated myself in the past, it's akin to being the master of a slave. I cringe at the thought of anyone being treated the way slaves have been treated in the past, and although not physically violent to myself, I used to push and push myself until I dropped – and I have become physically incapable of continuing on. I have criticized myself harshly – which I visualize as self-flagellation of the spirit and I have told myself that I would never measure up to those I admire most. In other aspects of our lives, perhaps we don't push ourselves at all because we don't think we're worth it, we eat badly, we don't exercise, we don't allow ourselves to dream and we merely trudge through the treacle of our bland existence until our time is up – chained to the daily grind of life and the obligations of serving others. What on earth is that about? And what a waste of life!

Mindfulness is a necessary partner of self-compassion – we need to be aware of how we talk to ourselves and counter the negative self-talk with more caring and kind words. For example – instead of saying "God you're hopeless!" when you forget where you've put something, say " I must have been busy when I put that down, I'm sure I'll find it!" and congratulate yourself when you do. Start to accept compliments and be grateful for them, instead of throwing it back in the face of the person who complimented you with automatic retorts such as: " Oh, it's nothing really", "But I still look old" or "Anyone can do that" etc. etc. Just learn to say thank you and appreciate the thought.

Kindness is being gentle and considerate; when we're being kind towards others, we are being thoughtful and considerate, giving attention to someone without harm. Are you kind towards yourself?

Not surprisingly, self-compassion really arises out of love and leaves judgement out of the equation. It's important to drop the notion of whether or not you deserve compassion (clearly from our own behaviour we generally don't believe we do); it's about getting on with it and practicing it routinely anyway. So how do we do that? Where do we start? We can practice self-compassion when we make mistakes, when we feel lonely, when we feel down, simply by telling ourselves that these are all normal parts of life for everyone, by telling ourselves that we are not unique in this human and life experience. Once we start to believe and understand this, we find a greater connection with ourselves and with the rest of humanity. It seems so easy to feel hard done by on one hand, believing others should help us more and at the same time not feel worthy of giving ourselves the comfort we need – paradoxical isn't it. How does that happen? That doesn't even make sense once you write it down. That type of thought process comes from self-pity, not self-compassion!

We like to feel in general that we are above average in everything we do. And society values us being above average – we expect it in work appraisals, fitness assessments, job promotions, winning awards. Well it's a bit of predicament that we get ourselves into here. Of course it is important to try your hardest to be your best self and to be your best at what you are applying your effort at, but it's also okay to accept where you're at, where you land. Having the expectation of being above average is strong in our society, but if everyone were above average, then it wouldn't be above average would it? We wouldn't have any more bell curves, we would just have a straight line, and where's the fun in that? There would be no room for improvement in anything, and I personally feel the happiest when I'm learning new things.

Kristen Neff has a wonderful exercise where you sit and contemplate two things you consider yourself to be above average at, two things you are average at and two things you are below average at. Sitting and connecting with the feelings that arise with these realizations is important in establishing where you're at right now and that this is perfectly okay. All through our lives we have learned and grown through experience, from babies to toddlers – learning new physical, motor and social skills, from toddler to pre-school age and throughout school life there is massive learning and growth in an academic, social and physical sense. This growth in learning doesn't stop when we finish school; we continue to learn from many experiences everyday, even if we don't consciously acknowledge this. Taking some time out to reflect on our day is an important part of self-compassion where we can see how the experiences have impacted our lives.

We need to slow down to grow faster. We need to search within ourselves so we can give to others. We don't all have to aspire to be the Dalai Lama, but every single one of us has something important to say and something worthy of sharing. We are connected as humans who are sharing the planet in a communal experience; we are not individuals going about our own day in a bubble.

The ripple effect is real and you have the opportunity to impact people every time you speak or interact with someone. Simply smiling and engaging with the person waiting in line with you will change the experience of their day. Their attitude will be different based on that interaction and will affect the interactions they have with others – which in turn will influence the interactions those people will have with others and so on ...

Starting by being kinder and thankful and grateful to yourself will change the way you see yourself interacting with those around you. It needs to start with you (and it's fun!).

It is so simple to see this ripple effect, particularly in your own family life, - in fact you can conduct your own experiment here – be more light-hearted in yourself, treat yourself with less judgement and see how those around you respond. Maybe you'll be able to help others be less harsh on themselves too. No doubt you've seen the ripple effect of being unkind or harsh to a child and seeing the effect that has on their interactions with those around them, the opposite is also very true!

Communication, real communication – face to face, even

verbal communication on the telephone makes a huge impact. Remembering to call someone, maybe just calling people out of the blue to see how they are – with no strings attached, is a rare commodity these days. When was the last time someone called you just to see how you are going? When was the last time you did this for someone else? When was the last time you checked in with yourself and asked yourself how you're going?

You can use the centering/feelings meditation we have done already to check in like this daily, starting with the simple question - "How am I feeling today?" – and pay attention to the answers!

You can use affirmations here too "I am happy, I am well, I am peaceful, I find joy, I am kind, I am worthy". If you are a person who takes more notice of what others say to you, you can add to these affirmations by adding "You, Marion Turner are happy, She, Marion Turner is happy" and so on. Try looking in the mirror and really looking at yourself, look at yourself in the eye and ask how you are feeling, what are you looking forward to today? Pop the book down for a moment and go and do that right now. If you don't have a mirror, use the camera in your phone, to really look and engage with you.

When you wake up in the morning, say good morning to yourself, repeat your affirmations silently in your head while you lay in bed, and start your day with gentle guidance and compassion. I like to do spend a few minutes awake in bed, doing just that, feeling gratitude for being here, for what the day will bring and to say good morning to myself.

But what if you are really struggling with starting to love yourself? How do you move forward from here?

If you really can't feel it – start by taking the steps towards loving yourself – for example, one thing on your list may be to give yourself time to meditate daily, to eat better, to start exercising, and definitely add some things from your nourishing list. Let yourself lighten up and enjoy the day. Try sitting down, acknowledging how you are feeling right now, and just repeating to yourself "I love you". Leave space so you can feel what physical sensations may arise in your body, then repeat and wait. Continue for as long as you feel comfortable doing it.

Learn to let go of what (you think) others think of you, it's great to love yourself, it's great to do things for yourself. Often the people who are critical of you spending time on yourself are basically reflecting a lack in their own lives and they are most likely jealous.

A big part of loving yourself is being able to receive love from others. That can be as simple as starting to accept compliments graciously and simply saying thank you, instead of making excuses or down playing the compliment as we discussed before. A compliment is a verbal gift. If someone gave you a physical gift, how would you accept that? Most likely you would smile and say thank you, you certainly wouldn't be throwing it back in their face. When you reject or deflect a compliment, you are rejecting a gift from someone. If you find it hard to accept compliments, simply start by saying "thank you" – for the other person's sake at least, until you feel comfortable with it.

As soon as we start to treat ourselves with compassion, we start to dissolve the disconnect between others and ourselves as we finally start to treat ourselves with the same love and compassion we extend to others. Suffering is not an essential part of life; you don't have to earn all your rewards through hardship. Do you really wish for your children to have a hard life, or are you trying your best to make their lives easier for them? Why don't we believe we deserve the same?

We are allowed to be happy and we are allowed to love ourselves. Once you establish your love for yourself, you can start to forgive your mistakes, accept your mistakes and release yourself from guilt and shame.

You have to create change if you want things to be different – so you can start right now!

Beginning a daily self-compassion practice is essential to re-connecting with yourself through love. Following s simple feelings (centering meditation) that we went through earlier, with a self-compassion meditation works wonders for me. I repeat phrases to myself that I wish someone else would say to me – or that I would wish for someone else, such as – "May I be happy" "May I be well", "May I be peaceful", "May I find joy" … Also, the invocation meditation I have included in this chapter, is a great segue into feeling love in a physical and spiritual sense.

Invocation Meditation (Dr Ian Gawler)

Now imagine, as if it were in the sky above you, the highest source of power that you know ... the embodiment of your own truth ... it may be an image that for you symbolizes God, or it may be the figure of Christ, Mother Mary or a particular Saint ... or it may be a figure from another tradition ... or you may prefer a more abstract image such as the sun which could represent the source of Universal Energy ...

Whichever of these symbolic images you find most helpful ... imagine that as well as a source of energy ... this is a source of love and compassion ... of loving kindness ... of a presence that has your own best interest at heart ...

As this image forms in your mind ... allow yourself to imagine what it would feel like to come into the presence of this Divine Source of Energy ... What would it be like to feel yourself in the presence of God? ... Or Christ? ... Or the figure that embodies truth for you? ... Or the source of Universal Energy? ...

Sometimes as you feel yourself coming closer to that presence ... you may wish to say something ... a prayer ... an explanation ... a request ... sometimes, something may be said to you or for you ... so you could listen for that...

Once you feel this Divine presence as if it is in the sky above you ... imagine that a beam of white light begins to flow from its very centre, down towards you ... an outpouring of energy and loving kindness ... if you are focussed upon a figure ... imagine this light flowing from its very heart ... if you are using the sun, imagine the shaft of light flowing from its very centre ... Now as this beam of warm, liquid, white light reaches your head ... it not only flows down around your body ... but also it flows through your body ... warm ... liquid ... white light ... slowly flowing down through your body ... almost like water filtering down through dry sand ...

Warm liquid white light ... flowing from that infinite source ... and flowing down through every part of your body ... like having a wash on the inside ... it washes away anything old or worn or unwanted ... anything you want to be free of ... are ready to let go of ... from your body ... in your emotional life ... from your mind ... anything you want to be free of ... like having a wash on the inside ...

And also, this warm, liquid, white light, brings with it a new energy ... a sense of vitality ... a sense of healing and wholeness ... you can feel it filling your body and your being ...

You may see this quite visually or you may have it as a feeling experience ... like feeling a flow of energy ... or a sensation of warmth moving down through your body ...

When the light does flow down to the ends of your arms ... it will flow out through the end of the fingers ... when it does reach the end of your legs ... it will flow out through the feet ... washing away with it anything old, or worn or unwanted ...

When this light comes to any difficult, tense, painful or blocked areas ... it simply washes through them ... clearing them ... relaxing them ... letting them go ... You may see the affected area as having a particular shape ... maybe a particular colour ... when the light reaches such an area ... you may see that colour being washed away, like a stain being washed away from clothes held under running water ... you may see the area dissolving from the outside in ... Some people find it helpful to imagine the light being concentrated almost like a laser ... this then burns away the affected blockage ... either from the outside in or the inside out ...

See and feel this warm liquid light filling every part of your body ... and now, feel your body the same all over ... your body filled with the vigour ... the vitality ... the radiance of the warm liquid white light ... and as this feeling becomes all encompassing ... it is as if you merge with it ... almost as if you dissolve into the light ... you feel it through your body ... and your mind ... it is as if you become at one with it ... Given that it stems from a infinite source, this can feel like merging or reuniting with the infinite ... go with it ... feel it all through ... all through ...

Now simply resting in the presence of that light and the Infinite Energy it represents and carries.

Gap

And now, move your feet a little ... your hands a little ... and then, when you are ready ... just let your eyes open gently.

Workbook Activity

Let's examine what we do for other people because we love them.

Write down a couple of names in your workbook and write down some of the things you do for them, wish for them, say to them, and give to them because you love them.

Now – write a list of things you do for yourself that show you love yourself. (If you can't think of anything, remember you are reading this book – so that should be on your list at the very least!)

Now – write a list of things you could do for yourself if you loved yourself.

Write a simple affirmation of love for yourself. One you can remember and continue to repeat often during the day.

A lovely way to finish this chapter is to do some free writing – give yourself 15 minutes or so, and just write what comes into your head. Perhaps do as Tracy led me to do and ask yourself the question "What does Spirit/God think of me?" If you do not feel a connection with a higher source, ask yourself "What do I have to offer?" and start there. When you do this type of writing, don't edit it as you go, just leave it to flow and keep it. It is a wonderful thing to look back on.

Chapter 7

Forgiveness

"Forgiveness is the fragrance that the violet sheds on the heel that has crushed it."
Mark Twain

Forgiveness is easier to say than it is to action! In order to forgive, you really have to be willing to let go. Resentment, anger, blame and bitterness all contrive to create a cycle of living in the past. Sometimes we try to hold someone to account for the problems in our lives. In reality, it is our reaction to the actions of others that create our circumstances. Does holding onto this emotional anchor really benefit us? Even if you are right, even if they did behave badly or hurt you, how are holding negative thoughts and ill feelings towards someone else helping you? What we do know is that what you are doing by staying in this cycle is activating your sympathetic nervous system. Your thoughts change your physiology. The stress caused by these negative thoughts is increasing the adrenalin and cortisol circulating through your body and keeping you running around the same old circular racetrack – when you entered the racetrack there was a beginning (and a potential finish line), but you've been running around it for so long, there's no end in sight, it's never ending.

But there is an end, the light can come on to signal the last lap and you can finally rest. You can get off the horse, drop the reins and walk away. And you can walk away tall and proud, seeking your next adventure and start living in the present. And the interesting thing is once you begin to delve into discovering who you need to forgive, you may be surprised to see who is on the list!

It's important to recognise that forgiveness does not condone the behaviour of others; it is an acceptance of what has happened and a green light for *you* to move on. You can even have gratitude for what you have learned and how you have grown through the experience. Even the intolerable people in our lives are gifts, they show us how we can change our behaviour and adapt to our ever changing world. When we forgive, we learn we can act with kindness and compassion in the face of unkindness. What a great gift that is for us to receive!

Holding onto grudges can create physical issues as well as emotional issues, it can create dis-ease and we have the power to turn that around through forgiveness and compassion. In his book Gray Matter (2011), Dr David Levy shows how forgiveness has resolved the maladies of many of his patients.

But often, the very thought of forgiveness makes people activate their resistance shield. "Why should I forgive them when it was them that caused …" and so on. Does this sound familiar? You know you've already tried it this way for sometime now, so how has that been working for you? Are you ready to try to change?

You may be concerned about discussing the forgiveness process with the person you are forgiving – do you have to do that? Absolutely not, the process is for you, not for them, so you can choose to have a conversation or not, it's up to you.

Simply bringing yourself back once more to the love and fear basis of emotions – it's easy to recognise that when we are holding a grudge, our sponsoring emotion is fear.

Alan Cohen in his book *A Course In Miracles Made Easy* – tells us "no-one or no-thing has the right to take away to take away your happiness – which is your birth-right – which is everyone's birth-right."

When we allow someone to take away our happiness, we are giving our power away. And it's important to know that when we are truly operating from love, we can't act from the fear state at the same time. So when you are truly happy with how you are yourself and how you are within yourself, no-one can make you feel bad. It follows then that when we are truly at peace and in love with ourselves, no-one and no-thing can take that away from us. Have you let someone take away your happiness? Have you given your power away?

As discussed in the last chapter, one of the biggest fears we face is that we are unworthy or inadequate. As long as we hold onto either one of those beliefs, we cannot escape the fear state. The truth is every single one of us is worthy and adequate; we are all just different. We need to create belief in ourselves to establish our worthiness and from there we can escape fear.

"Comparison is the death of joy."
Mark Twain

We are all different but in essence we are the same. We are

individuals, all unique in our own right but we are all connected on this planet. Unfortunately we allow comparison of ourselves with others to lead to feelings of unworthiness in ourselves. On the flipside, we can sometimes compare ourselves with others from a perspective of superiority – where we would never behave as others have, we would never say the things others say to us, we would never make those mistakes! Commonly, and unfortunately, we often fail to observe situations from another's viewpoint. The truth is, we don't know anyone else's truth. We assume other people's lives are happy and perfect (which makes us feel inadequate), or conversely, we may assume they have no morals and are purposefully hurtful towards us. When we think beyond our "inadequacies" and truly consider the other person's situation without judgement but rather through exploring the possibilities of what might have possibly happened in their lives, we become more connected to others and we become compassionate. And this compassion can be extended to the person we need to forgive.

So how do we start forgiving people? A good place to start is trying to find something to like about someone who has wronged us. How about the irritating relation that always has to put down what you are doing? The person who always has to have a snide comment about how much time you have off work? Can you think of something that you can be grateful for about that person? Even if it was one time they complimented you or gave you a nice present? If that's not possible for you, maybe you can look at how they may have been treated by others in the past and find some compassion for them. What happens if you picture them as a small child, can you feel love for them before you even knew them? Can you start to see them through different eyes? I think I'd be pretty accurate in saying that all babies are born with pure innocence, imagining the wrong-doer as a new-born would surely stir some compassion in most people.

I remember feeling hurt when I heard my sister-in-law was getting remarried some years after the death of my brother. Even still, at this point down the track, I was being quite petulant and thinking to myself (and definitely not voicing it to anyone else) "Great, you get to move on and get a new husband, I can never replace a brother!" It was like I was blaming her for me being stuck where I was. Of course I never said that to her, and I offered my congratulations at the time of the wedding but deep down I still felt hurt, and possibly in retrospect, envious of her ability to move on with her life. I was comparing her journey to mine, which was never going to be the same; the relationship with a brother is not the same as the relationship with a husband (neither is superior of course, they are just different). I was wrongly assuming that she didn't love him as much as I did, that I would never consider remarrying if I lost my husband – all ridiculous comparisons and commentary that was rooted in fear. I didn't know how to move forward so I assumed no-one else should be moving forward either.

When I initially thought about forgiving people, I felt I had to forgive Fiona for moving forward with her life. When I thought about this more deeply, I found I really needed to forgive myself for feeling this way towards Fiona. I became compassionate towards myself – a big tick! I had no prior experience with navigating through all of this and I was learning. Thank God I was learning! I was high up on my forgiveness list.

It's important to know that holding onto stress and resentment will hurt you, not feeling your feelings will hurt you too. I'll tell you another personal story in the hope you may be able to relate to something similar in your situation. Around four to five months after Mostyn's passing I was suffering from a serious bout of lumbar pain. I was having difficulty moving and changing positions, getting dressed was certainly a challenge. I could sit down but then getting back up was excruciating. One particular Sunday afternoon, my Mum rang. She really just rang for a chat and then mentioned that she was going to my brother Gary's house for dinner that night. She asked if I was going. "We hadn't been invited" I said, and promptly burst into uncontrollable sobbing. I knew it wasn't about the dinner invitation (there was no caveat in place that we must accompany Mum and Dad to my brother's house every time they visited!) but I could not stop crying. My husband heard me and came into the room, took the phone and told Mum I was okay, that I would ring her later. Of course I was not okay and that was a ridiculous thing to say (and it was said at my prompting). I cried and cried for nearly two hours. I had not sobbed like that since I could remember. It was seriously unstoppable. When I did stop, I was exhausted. I got up out of the chair and my back pain had gone completely!

As a physiotherapist, I had trouble really connecting with people's inference that they held their stress in their neck or their back – I used to explain it by suggesting it was just increased muscle tension. Since this episode however, I absolutely recognise this in my patients and I believe part of the reason for this – if it needs to be explained scientifically – could be related to adrenal overload. This was just one of the physical manifestations of my grief that I came to recognise over the years. There are many similar stories that people have reported that have resolved once they have been through a process of forgiveness. While I didn't identify this process as forgiveness at the time, now I can see that through this, I forgave my brother Gary for having my parents over for dinner (this sounds so ridiculous now), I forgave myself for holding a ridiculous assumption that I was being left out, I forgave my mum for telling me she was going there!

Initially when I started crying, I was thinking – if she didn't ring me, I wouldn't have known and I wouldn't have started crying! As I write it now it sounds absurd, absurd but true. Maybe you have similar stories in your journey. Please don't feel you have to have a monumentous event to forgive someone for – the purpose of telling you this story is that sometimes we really need to forgive and let go of all the little things too!

Getting back to intentional forgiveness, it's time to let go of those people who are tangled up in your life like chewing gum tangled up in your hair. You know it might be messy getting rid of it, it may even hurt a little, but you need to cut the ties, you need to let others be who they are. It is not up to you to control what others do, how others think; you can't change them but you can give yourself the freedom to let go. You can choose to feel better about yourself and cutting those ties can be done through forgiveness. Again it's about letting go the struggle, letting go of the resistance, allowing the flow to be restored. And with that flow comes love, peace and joy.

So where do you start? Sometimes situations become more awkward the longer they are left unsaid. We start to ruminate and create more fiction and imaginings around the situation so it becomes untenable to mention at all, and we may assume the other person is doing the same – they may be, but they may also be oblivious to what you're concerned about. If it's a situation that you really need some clarity around, don't be scared to ask someone difficult questions – it might only be you that feels uncomfortable, maybe asking and getting clarity is enough for you to find the avenue for forgiveness. If you don't feel brave enough to talk to someone over the phone, maybe send them a letter or email to find the answers you are seeking.

Don't forget that maybe they want to talk too. People commonly make the mistake of not talking to others in case they upset them; really what you are doing is denying them someone to talk to as well. I feel this is something I have denied my family up until now. I really felt I didn't want to upset anyone by bringing things up, but it certainly does deny others the chance to communicate how they are feeling.

When you find yourself on your own forgiveness list, don't be too harsh on yourself. When judging yourself on past behaviour, remember you acted on what you knew at the time. You are now judging your past behaviour based on what you know now – that is so unfair. Would you chastise your three-year old child because he can't answer an algebra question – when he hasn't learned the math? How could he possibly know if he hasn't learned that yet? It's the same for us now; we didn't know what we know now back then. So we should reflect on our past with kindness and awareness of where we were at the time.

It's also the same for other people who have wronged us; perhaps they haven't learned what we have learned yet. We can apply this compassion to others also.

Some of the situations that have been commonly brought up for discussion in the *From Grief to Gratitude* workshop regarding forgiveness are: arguments that were had, the last things people said to the person who passed away, not being loving enough in relationships which have failed, not understanding the needs of other people and more. Some also say they have already done it, they have "let that person go out of their life" but the way in which it's said shows so much attachment to the situation still, that they haven't truly let go.

Regarding self-forgiveness, a common issue that comes up through discussion in the workshops is not being present at the time a loved one passes. It's a common story that they have been by their loved one's side for hours or days (or longer), only to miss the passing when they went to have a shower or to grab something to eat. This discussion inevitably turns around to acknowledging that perhaps some people want to pass with fewer people around, or no-one there – maybe that's happened as they wished it to. Maybe some people want company when they pass, maybe some don't. Again, this is not something we can control; we can only control our response or our reaction towards it.

Some participants report they feel guilt because they only got to the bedside after their loved one could no longer communicate with them. It seems we look for anything to make us complicit in the mess we have created for ourselves, like it is our fault. Others report the loved one planning to pass, having said all their goodbyes and then are disappointed in the morning when they are still here! On the other hand, some of us don't get a chance to say goodbye, some loved ones pass away completely unexpectedly, like Moz did. There is no right or wrong to any of this, it is just how it is – it is a situation to acknowledge and accept.

I really think the lesson in this is to live our lives as lovingly and honestly as we can, care for all those around us, and when others pass happen, as they will continue to do, we can rest comfortably in the knowledge that we have lived and loved well.

When considering the loss of a relationship with someone, it is important to realise that it may be time for you to let them and the relationship go. Of course if you are grieving the situation, it's highly likely that this is not the ideal situation for you, but again, as with the passing of someone you have loved, it's not always your decision. If someone holds a particular point of view very strongly, it is really only up to them to change this if they wish to. Clearly if you are grieving it, you must have loved the person in that relationship at some point, think back to the version of that person you loved, feel compassion for that person and let go. Forgiveness will bring you release and relief, it will allow you to move forward and make space for new opportunities in your life. If you are still holding onto the misgivings, the bitterness, you are denying yourself the opportunity to really begin to love yourself. Forgiveness requires compassion for yourself as well as the other party. It's time to give yourself a break and start really living your life.

I hadn't supported Fiona as I felt I should have after Mostyn's passing, but I just wasn't in the space to do that at the time, it is a regret of mine but something I have forgiven myself for as I have found compassion for myself in that situation. Fiona has been extremely gracious to me and helped me with writing this book; she has helped me with information I requested and for continuing to be a loving sister-in-law. We have had a very long connection which pre-dated Mostyn and Fiona's marriage by many years and those valuable relationships are worth holding onto.

It's so important to realise and accept that everyone's story around an incident is different. Everyone has been affected differently, because everyone has had a different experience – based on their relationships, circumstances, knowledge of what has happened in the past and more. Just as our experience is the truth to us, so is everyone else's to them. We need to dig deep and find that compassion and perspective to allow our understanding and acceptance to grow. While we may continue to find out more information as time passes, it's likely we will never have the complete picture from all perspectives – but we can accept that ours is not the only view.

Perhaps it's an argument (or many) that has resulted in the loss of a relationship that you are grieving. Perhaps we are grieving the loss of relationships as well as the passing of a loved one. It gets complicated, so many relationships are intertwined in these situations and we need to give ourselves space to really pull them apart and find out what's really eating at us. We need to remember that we can only control our own behaviours and reactions and choices, not those of others. We also need to remember that we don't know the full truth of what has gone on in the life of the other person with whom we've lost the relationship. We may think we do, particularly if it's a spouse, parent or sibling. But do we really? We haven't been around for everything that has happened in the life of that person, we haven't heard everything that has been said to them since they were born (and perhaps before they were born). We weren't in the classroom hearing what the teachers said to them, what their siblings said to them, the throw away comments that were not intended to harm but have ended up scarring them, leaving them with beliefs that perhaps they are not worthy of love, inadequate and so on. We cannot pretend to know. All we know is that they acted with the knowledge they had at the time. Is that not enough to be able to forgive someone, to let their hold over you go?

It doesn't mean they treated you fairly or well, it just means that you understand there is more to their story than you know.

Ideally forgiveness will be unconditional, you're not going to forgive on the condition the other person does something to appease you, this takes the power of forgiveness out of your hands. You alone have the power to forgive someone and let go of the hurt, anger, sadness, and frustration. You have the ability to simply accept what has happened – because it has happened – this doesn't mean it's right or you condone it, you have simply accepted it has happened. When you can find in your heart some compassion for a part of that person's life, you can concentrate on that and let yourself heal. Can you find it in your heart to find compassion for that person as a baby, or as a child? Maybe you can try to walk in their shoes and imagine living through their childhood, identifying with problems they have in their life.

I absolutely believe that holding onto so many issues without talking about them – created my oesophageal ulcers – I believe this was a combination of stress and physical manifestation of the inability to process my grief and to allow my heart to heal. I was unable to feel energy flow through this area in meditations – I couldn't sense physical sensations below my heart while meditating, I was unable to visualise light or water flowing through my chest and into my abdomen. This blocked toxic energy literally started eating away at me. We even describe these effects in our language with phrases like: What's eating at you? Or who is eating at you? I believe for me it was the combination of my inability to let go of issues, and my inability to "feel my feelings" – to let go of the resistance I was unconsciously harbouring that literally started to eat at me. I have forgiven myself for not knowing this!

As we've discussed before, the stories we hold onto might not be the truth. For example – in one workshop, a participant discussed the absence of photos of the loved one who had passed in his family home. There were photos of animals and other family members but none of her loved one. This participant had concluded that this showed the family did not really love him as much as other members of the family or the pets. But what other possible truths could there be in this situation?

Well, perhaps that person didn't like having photos of him on display, maybe the spouse had taken them down because she couldn't handle seeing the photos at this time, or maybe he was the photographer and was keen on taking photos of everyone else. Maybe you can think of other scenarios for this situation. This is a useful exercise to do with your own situation, write it down and then think of other possible alternatives, stand back as a neutral observer, leave your feelings at the door and be objective. This can really help in releasing some of your tightly held fear-based emotions when you see things with clarity and objectivity. Sometimes we need to acknowledge that we need to let go of the need to be right all the time. You may be right but how is that working for you at the moment? Does it matter?

Simply writing a letter explaining your hurt and your need to release everything can be cathartic – you don't necessarily need to send this letter (and maybe you can't – maybe you need to write it for the person who has passed), you could burn the letter and feel the release as the words go up in flames.

One participant, Shannon, reported writing a letter to her mother who had passed, in it she had mentioned some things she had been holding onto and needed to say. She lit the paper and is not sure why, but she put out the flames before it was fully burned. To her surprise, five pieces of paper remained – the words left on those five pieces of paper were "Dad" "I love you Mum", "she just needs self love", "be happy" "heal" "Hudson". She has kept these pieces of paper as a sign that her message was received with love and feels such a connection when she revisits them.

It's important to realise that this forgiveness process is for you - the other person doesn't need to know you have forgiven them, you could write a letter and choose to send it or not, or to burn it. Perhaps the issue lies with you more than the other person and it may not be in their best interest to let them know you have forgiven them; they may have been completely unaware of the situation, and creating pain for them is unnecessary. Perhaps you could write them a different letter, expressing gratitude for having them in our life rather than explaining what you have been hanging onto. If someone has treated you badly, you may not ever wish to talk or communicate with him or her again in any form. That's fine, just perform the forgiveness for yourself, there is no compunction to involve them in it in anyway but you will certainly feel better for it. You will find when you have truly forgiven, no angst arises when you bring them to mind, as you have let that go, you will feel neutral or loving.

So there are many different ways to practice forgiveness, you can visualize yourself hugging the other person, you can visualize yourself cutting ties, you can write letters that you can send, keep or burn, you can visualize yourself walking in their shoes. The end result is the same, you let go and move on with love in your heart. The meditation at the end of this chapter is a wonderful meditation called loving kindness. If you find this difficult to do the first time, don't be discouraged, it can take practice, please try it a few times to see if you can progress with it.

As we start to practice forgiveness, we enter new situations with a different awareness and mindfulness regarding our ability to choose how we react to situations from the outset.

Workbook Activity

Let's start with a list of people that immediately come to mind when you consider forgiveness and letting go of hurtful situations. Make a list of people you feel you need to forgive right now, next to their names, explain what you think you need to forgive them for. You may find yourself on this list and that is quite normal. Feelings of personal shame and guilt can be worked through with self-forgiveness, releasing the past and moving forward. If you imagine driving a car forward with your vision focused on the rear-view mirror, you know it's only a matter of time before you have an accident or create chaos. Start to focus your intention on the present moment and looking forward so you can deal with what's happening right now. That's all that matters, that's all that's known.

Pick one person that you want to work on right now.

There may be resistance to thinking about this, to even thinking about some of these people at all. You may also be surprised to find people popping into your mind that you thought you had forgiven some time ago, so maybe you need to work on forgiving them more. You may have said you've forgiven someone but didn't really let it go, there's a difference between what we say and what we actually do – the proof will be in the feelings that arise when that person is brought to mind.

You can now write some affirmations, such as "I, [your name], forgive [their name] for [...]. It's important to be specific here; this will help you to let go of the situation.

If you find this difficult, try starting with "I, [your name], am open to forgiving [their name] for [...]

In time, this may change to "I forgive myself for judging ...". Or perhaps you may wish to start with yourself. Remember the mirror exercise when we were talking about compassion? You can just look at yourself in the mirror and express your forgiveness directly – so you are hearing it, seeing it and feeling it as the giver and the receiver.

I love the way this meditation allows you to generate feelings of love, to receive love and give love, and to share love with others. It is certainly worth practicing; please don't give up on this if you find it difficult, it's the difficult things we need to persist with. I find this a great go to meditation if I feel someone is "getting under my skin"! I have used this meditation on myself as well, visualizing myself as a child. Have a look on the list you just wrote and pick just one person to start this practice with. The key to these meditations is to go with the flow, accept what turns up and allow it to happen. Each time you do this meditation, it will be different.

Loving Kindness Meditation (Dr Ian Gawler)

Take up your position, relax physically ...

Imagine as if they were sitting in front of you, the person who has loved you most in life ... traditionally your mother is recommended, but if that is not so easy, recall a person and a time when you felt deeply loved ... most importantly recall the feeling ... this person's unconditional positive regard for you ... their love ... their acceptance ... their warmth ... Give yourself over to those feelings ... The aim is to build the feeling of loving kindness as strongly and clearly as you can ... and as you feel that love rising within your heart, return the loving feeling to this precious person ... Return the love as if you are radiating it back to them ...

You may well find it helpful to visualise the loving kindness in the form of white light ... to see this light glowing in the heart of the person who loved you most ... for that light to become stronger and brighter ... and then to radiate out like a searchlight ... A beam of light... that travels to your heart ... then this white light fills your heart before radiating out and filling your entire body ... perhaps even wrapping around you like a cloak or blanket ...

As you feel yourself filled with the warmth and comfort of this radiant, white light ... you imagine broadcasting it back from your heart to the heart of the person who loved you the most ... Then you continue this back and forwards exchange of the light until you have the sense that both of you are filled with loving kindness ...

Now imagine a neutral person in your life ... as if they were sitting on the right of the person who loved you most... This may be a person who you know quite casually, but who you know well enough to bring to mind clearly ... As you imagine them in front of you ... have the intention of radiating those same feelings of loving kindness to them in the form of white light ...

Return to the person who loved you most ... rekindle, rebuild the feelings of loving kindness you felt from them ... feel it again all through your body ... and then project that feeling through the vehicle of white light to the neutral person. Keep doing this, moving from one to the other, until you feel the neutral person is as filled with white light and loving kindness as are you and the person who loved you most ... Imagine this neutral person feeling filled with loving kindness ...

Again, you may do this in a feeling sense, radiating the feeling to them and feeling it wrapping all around and through them, warming their heart and filling them with loving kindness ... however, you may also find it helpful to visualise the loving kindness in the form of white light welling up in the heart of the person who loved you the most ... to feel that light flowing into your own heart ... filling your own body ... and then radiating it out like a search light, a beam of light that travels from your heart to the neutral person's heart ... then it fills the neutral person's heart with the same clear white light before radiating out and filling their entire body ... perhaps even wrapping around them like a cloak or blanket.

Now imagine a person who has been difficult in your life as if they are sitting before you on the right of the neutral person ... project the same white light and feelings of loving kindness to them; starting by returning to the person who loved you the most ... re-establish the flow of white light and the feelings of loving kindness to yourself ... and then radiating them to the difficult person ...

Now, continue to alternate between the three people until the white light is glowing evenly in all three ... and the feelings within all three and yourself are the same ...

Now simply rest with the feelings of loving kindness ... almost as if you are absorbed in those feelings and the presence of the white light.

Gap

And now, move your feet a little... your hands a little... and then, when you are ready... just let your eyes open gently.

Chapter 8

Honouring Yourself and Finding Your Purpose

"He who has a why to live for can bear almost any how."
Friedrich Nietzsche

Is it possible to honour the life of someone else if you don't truly honour yourself? I don't think so. In fact honouring yourself is how you honour someone else's life because you are maximizing the potential of yours, not wasting the opportunities you have right now to live a wonderful and fulfilled life! Letting go of the grief is necessary for this to happen, for you to move forward. Letting go of the grief doesn't mean you don't miss who or what you have lost; it just means you have accepted it. Is there any other alternative? Not a productive one, I've tried the clinging option, and it didn't work for me and I'm sure it's not going to work for you either.

I guess the beauty of life is that we have contrasts. If we didn't know what darkness was, we wouldn't appreciate light. And so it is with grief. Once we let it go, we can really feel the change in ourselves. Sometimes we will still have moments of sadness, that's for sure, and that's not a failure. That is normal. Memories will resurface and because they are so strong, they have emotions embedded in them, so we can sometimes still feel the physical pull of those emotions all over again. But what we've learned so far is to know that we are shedding light on our awareness of our experience. This sadness is part of love, not fear I believe. Our self-compassion comes into play at these times when we realize we are sad again, we can notice this tenderly, accept that this is so, and gently move on without admonishment or derision, without thoughts of failure. Every time we notice what is coming our way, we are using our mindfulness skills, combining this with our compassion and the knowledge that we have the power to steer our own course.

Sometimes the wind changes, sailors know that. So they adjust their sails to accommodate this and stay on their path. We can do the same. We can gently nudge our focus to shift from sadness to gratitude.

When we cut the ties to our grief, we are creating space inside of ourselves for more joy. We find the room to experience happier memories of our loss, to treasure those memories as we treasured what is no longer with us.

Our world is constantly changing, our thoughts constantly change, the weather changes, the leaves on the trees change, everything ages over time until it's gone and is then replaced by something else which is never exactly the same. We can't press the pause button, but we can get invested in ourselves and invested in our lives, pick ourselves up and dust ourselves off.

We all have time left, we don't know how much but while we are breathing we have time. We need to honour our lives by making them the best they can be; by filling our cups and helping others do the same. Isn't that what life is about? Surely it's not about having the most expensive house(s), the latest car(s), all the material things that can't love you back? Surely it's about our experience of our world and the value we bring to it.

It doesn't matter what you do, you can make a difference in someone else's life by being the best you can be. And that value is often felt when you are being of service to others. This may come through your occupation, perhaps community or volunteer work, your ability to help those in your family, friends and neighborhood networks. Everyone is capable of being of service to others in some way, but you are truly only being of service when you do so with no reservations, no misgivings, no second thoughts and no resentment about what you are doing or why you are doing it!

But let's start with us first; how do we start to honour ourselves? We start by making choices that benefit us, we start to wake up and be conscious and come off the bench and start playing the game of our life. We need to get some focus in this world full of distractions and promises and dig deep to find out what it is that we are here for. And it will be different for everyone. Some are born to be surgeons, some are born to be entertainers, and some are born to build. Whatever you were born to be, you know deep inside what that is. It doesn't matter what anyone else thinks of this, it matters that you fulfill your promise to yourself and start doing what you need to be doing.

How do I know what I should be doing? That's a common question really. You only have to talk to teenagers in their final years of schooling to find that most of them have lost their way. If I had my time again, I would have video evidence of the things my children said they wanted to be when they were around three to four years of age. Before they cared what other people thought, before they realized how dog eat dog the world can be if you let it.

My son is 15 at the time of writing this book. He is extroverted, likes/loves acting depending on the day you ask at the moment; and he has a definite talent for it. As a little boy, he always wore super-hero costumes, he would wear them to the shops, to parties, anywhere. He wasn't necessarily loyal to one particular hero, but Spiderman, Superman, Ironman and Batman were probably his go to heroes. He even noted this himself and when we asked him what he wanted to be when he grew up he said he wanted to be part-time Spiderman, part-time Superman and part-time Ironman. He wanted a hover board and he wanted the Ben 10 Omnitrix (I think he had every available merchandise option of that). One day he asked us what job he could have that would let him do all these things, and shoot guns, and drive cars and ride horses. My husband told him an actor would get to do all of these things and more. So being an actor it was. Time will tell if he hangs onto this dream in his world of peer pressure. Our message to him has been clear, we will support him with whatever he wants to do, but don't let anyone tell you that you can't be an actor. I made the mistake of suggesting a few years back, that he might need a backup plan for acting in case the work wasn't steady. He would only have been around 10 years old at the time and he said to me "You don't have any faith in me, you don't think I can do it!" Wow, that was a slap in the face and really highlighted to me that the message I was sending him was exactly that. I completely retracted that statement, it was based on inherited beliefs from my own upbringing that made sure that you had to have a secure job at all times to be safe in the world. When I think back to what I imagined I would be doing as an adult, I always thought I would be living in a house in the hills, writing books from my office, looking out over the rolling landscape. I would also be travelling the world!

So there's something I can do about that. I lose track of time when I'm writing, when I'm in the flow, the words pour out and I'm not sure they're even coming from me. I take some comfort in this and hope that my words will help others and that this is part of my purpose in life. I feel deep down, my purpose is to help other people and I am doing that in all aspects of my working life and family life. This can be draining too, when you have spent all your energy helping others, sometimes you feel a little resentment because you don't have the time and energy for yourself. But there is a solution there – it's a conscious choice to decide how you spend your time. So I am now allocating time for some of the things I need to do for me. And it feels great. My past tells me I start a lot of things and don't finish, so I am concentrating on projects that I will finish before I start anything new. I'm also not trying to change everything at once, it's usually an instant fail for me when I do that. Instead, I am asking myself when I make a choice, is this in the best interests of my purpose and my life? That works for me.

So how do you know what your purpose is? Firstly, your contemplation meditation may have led to an insight for you. What I find helpful is looking at the things that nourish me, that bring me joy and that gives some indication of the space you feel most connected to. When you are doing something that feels that you never have enough time to do, when you look forward to getting up and starting that, when you are racing to get more done before you have to stop, when you lose track of time while you're doing it, these are all indicators that you're engaging with your purpose. You are actually happy on the inside, and that's where joy starts!

I had a conversation recently with someone who quit her office job of 14 years to work from home doing makeup and styling for weddings and other beauty services on a full-time basis. She told me that several people criticized her decision at the time, telling her that "that's not a real job", "you can't make a living from that". Guess what – she's doing very well thank you very much and she absolutely loves what she does. Don't let the dream-slayers keep you down!

Honouring yourself means honouring your purpose. So move over towards what lights you up, don't worry about what others may say about you – again, that is your ego trying to steer you away from trying something new and less secure. Who cares what other people think? Quite often the judgement from others is based on their own fear of change, of their beliefs that they are continuing to cling to. Be brave, let go, do what YOU need to do. Then you will be honouring yourself, then you will be fulfilling your purpose, then you will have fewer regrets on your deathbed. Are you likely to feel fulfilled at the end of your life because you raced around like a maniac doing lots of little unimportant things, and you feel you wasted your time?

Do you believe everyone on earth has a purpose or a reason to be here? Do you believe you don't? What makes you so special that you don't have something to share with everyone else on the planet? Your passion and your purpose are most likely inextricably linked.

Workbook Activity

Take a moment to consider this carefully.

You might like to take a few moments to write down what comes up for you when you consider:

1. I am happy when …
2. I wish I had more time to spend …
3. I really want to …
4. What did I want to be when I was young?
5. What is stopping me doing what I want to do?
6. If I had all the money in the world, what would my dream life look like?

From this, you can create your bucket list, some things that are important to you to have accomplished in your life. It will also help you to identify some blocks to achieving your happiness. Maybe you need to delve further into some personal development to discover what blocks you have and why, but if you can at least identify that you have some that are stopping you from doing what you want, then you are on the way to moving them out of your life. Financial commitments may not allow you to pursue your passion full time to start with, but can you trade some time from somewhere else in your life to do what you love?

Self-Compassion and Purpose Meditation (Marion Turner)

Sitting with an open and upright posture, with your eyes gently closed, your hands resting comfortably on your lap, take a few moments to slowly relax your body in the best way you know how. Perhaps taking 3 slow deep breaths will help, feeling the muscles softening and loosening on the outbreath, just letting go ...

So your letting go physically, let yourself let go emotionally - give yourself permission to be in this space, there is nothing else you need to be doing right now, nowhere else you need to be, just being here right now is perfect ...

Allow your attention to rest in the space in front of your closed eyes, this can be a focal point for stillness and observation, perhaps there are some colours or patterns here, mostly it's just dark.

Bringing your awareness to any sounds coming to you from a distance, from outside the room, noticing not judging, allowing the sounds to come and go ... and then to the sounds inside the room, connecting yourself with the present moment through the awareness of sound ...

Now bring to mind a moment where you felt happiness, it doesn't have to be a big moment, it could be the feeling you get on a beautiful spring day, listening to birds, or it could be an event where you were excited for someone else or just felt overwhelming peace and gratitude ... Whatever that moment is, watch it. Just watch it in your mind's eye and feel the feelings that come along with that; feel the physical sensations in the centre line, the feeling line of your body. Savour this feeling. Stay with this feeling and experience it for a minute or two ...

Remembering and experiencing this moment, visualise light growing in your heart, getting bigger with every breath you take in, the light fills your heart so much that it starts to spill out into the rest of your body, filling up your centre line first then spilling over into every part of your body, you may feel this as a gentle tingling/buzzing as you start to become aware of the life force within you...

So much light fills your body that it starts seeping out of your body so the edges of your body are becoming blurry and you are bathed and filled with this glorious white light.

As you sit filled with this glorious light, repeat your self-compassion phrases over and over to yourself, as if you are whispering into your ear. If you have no phrases, perhaps you can listen; listen for ones that come to you. Or you may like to start with I am worthy, I am loved, I feel love, I am love ...

Repeating your phrases over and over in your mind, basking in the light and the love....

You may like to see yourself as a younger child, and feel that love and compassion towards yourself as you do towards innocent young children, that's still you.

I am worthy ...I am loved ...I feel love ... I am love ...

Allow your face to soften and your mouth to turn up into a gentle smile as you repeat your self-compassion phrases to yourself,

Feel the warmth... feel the love ... giving you love ... and receiving the love.

If you feel your attention wandering, bring yourself back to your breath, the space in front of your closed eyes, the light in your heart, the light through your body, whispering your phrases in your ear.

Sit for awhile, bathed in this self-love and take the time to feel love and joy, and imagine yourself feeling truly fulfilled and purposeful, what images come to mind for you?

Where are you when you are doing this?

What can you see around you – close by and off in the distance?

And what sounds can you hear?

Are there any particular fragrances, odour or tastes associated with this for you?

And what can you feel? What is the temperature like, are there any sensations you can feel? Where do you feel the sensations? Are they in your limbs? Are they in the centre-line of your body? What do you feel when you are doing this?

See yourself as successful, as throwing your heart and soul into what you are doing and enjoying every single moment of it and sit with this image for awhile ...

As we bring this meditation to a close, bring your attention back to the sounds coming to you from outside and inside the room, take a few deep breaths, activate your hands and feet by wiggling them a little and when you are ready, slowly open your eyes.

You may like to write down what came to mind during this meditation and do this often – self-love and connection with purpose are integral parts of finding the joy in our lives!

Chapter 9

Gratitude

"Do not spoil what you have by desiring what you have not; remember that what you now have was once among the things you only hoped for."

Epicurus

To be in a state of gratitude you must be present, even if you are being grateful for something that happened in the past, you are experiencing gratitude right now.

How grateful are you for what you have now in your life? Are you someone who really finds deep down that she/he will be happy when …? Are you putting off gratitude until you have all your heart desires? The truth is, you can be happy right now. There are things in your life that you can be grateful for, you just need to acknowledge that. It's a change in perspective where you connect with all the little wonderful moments that we experience everyday, that don't even get enough attention to be swept under the carpet, they are simply passed by. There can be opportunities for growth and joy in every moment!

Gratitude is absolutely borne from love. When we are expressing gratitude, we are expressing appreciation for what is happening, what has happened and what may happen in the future. So if you are having difficulty with really feeling love, try feeling gratitude, it's love too.

Mindfulness is a brilliant way to explore gratitude and the meditation included here is a perfect way to explore the things you can be grateful for you in your life. Sure you have sadness, but there are still good things all around you if you care to take a look. Dwelling in the gratitude, shifts your perception and allows you to operate from love.

The simplest way to start practicing gratitude is to write down things that you are grateful for. They don't have to be monumental occurrences, perhaps you are grateful for the beautiful blue sky out the window, the birds singing in the background, for your favourite jumper, for your cup of tea, for having running water, for having a heater to warm your house, for having a roof over your head, for having wonderful people in your life, for the smile the shop attendant gave you today, for the chance to experience another day …

Honestly, the list is endless. Being grateful for what you have right now, affirms your presence in your current situation and stops the wishing; it stops the wanting things to be different cycle that grief can tip us into.

Try recording three things you are grateful for before you begin your day and three at the end of the day. Doing so shifts you into the gratitude space, and starting the day this way, will have you notice things you may otherwise take for granted. For example, you may appreciate the surly teenager grunt as he greets you in the morning and be grateful he acknowledges you, you may look at him through different eyes and notice how tall he is getting, how handsome he is. You may pay more attention to your partner when he hands you a cup of coffee or tea in the morning and take the time to say thank you. You may look at your daughter studying, exercising and working and appreciate how hard she is working. Similarly, before you go to sleep, you will reflect on three things that happened during the day that you were grateful for. A beautiful way to enter sleep!

One *From Grief to Gratitude* participant shared how she committed to doing this many years ago and found her journal recently when moving and was amazed when she read through it. She also found one her departed husband had written – she had encouraged him to do this at the time but never knew he was keeping one. Rather than being sad when she discovered the journal, she felt this was a gift to her, not only reading the gratitude lists and statements in the journal, but knowing that her suggestion had helped to bring him some joy during life as well – here is the ripple effect in action.

Another way to express gratitude is to go out of your way to say thank you to people who help you. Even sending a text message or email to thank a friend for being there for you, start sending out the love and feel it come right back to you. Start to surround yourself in a blanket of warmth.

Workbook Activity

1. In your workbook, start by making a list of 10 things you can be grateful for right now! Alternatively, you can start a gratitude journal.

Leave a couple of pages here because you can add to this list every day

2. Now write three to five things you can be grateful for what you have lost. For example, personally, I am grateful for the stories I hear from others about Mostyn, I am grateful for the wonderful memories I have and for the joy he brought to the family.
3. Write a list of what you have learned through your lost. Perhaps you have delved into personal development that you would not otherwise have looked at, you have learned more about yourself, you have learned the importance of appreciating people while they are here, and so on … This list will continue to grow as you continue to be courageous and work your way through your grief, you will come to know you – and perhaps you had lost yourself a long time ago anyway and now you are developing the sense of purpose you need to live a more fulfilled life.

There is always a silver lining and sometimes you don't have to look that hard to find it. And yes, it's okay to find one. You are supposed to be enjoying your life, denying yourself joy is denying yourself love; it is not honouring yourself or you life, or what you have lost.

So getting back to loving yourself, perhaps starting with simple gratitude for other things in your life will help you to remember what it's like to look at life through the eyes of love.

Remember, gratitude is present, grief is past. Coming from love, will stop fear creeping in again, gratitude is like a switch we can use in a practical sense to move from fear to love.

To repeat again - gratitude allows love back into your life – we start to experience peace, contentment and joy. Through this process, we can come to accept our current situation (which will change with every moment). When we truly accept, we let go of the "if only's" and "what if's" - allowing you to release grief and fear. It allows you to release the fear associated with moving on. For many there is a real fear of letting go in case this might create a sense or feeling that you didn't really care. This is so far from the truth. I know feel that I am honouring my life and Mostyn's life as I have now found joy and purpose because I have come to know myself and love myself. I am making changes in my life that I couldn't be bothered making before, I didn't care enough about me to create a life I deserve, but now I do. The feeling of peace and serenity is absolutely beautiful. Honouring others lives through grace, joy, and a real sense of being you is so much more purposeful than creating busy-ness which denies you the capacity to be you.

If I hadn't lost Mostyn then, I wouldn't be where I am now. I didn't stop loving myself because he died, that had happened a long time before that. If Mostyn hadn't passed, who knows if I would have ever bothered to start to take care of me? It started such a long process of self discovery that I wonder now, would I have bothered becoming a meditation teacher, of pursuing so much personal development, of getting on to my writing? I will never know but I am grateful for the path I am on. This change has really flowed for me – once I dropped my resistance and fear of change, my fear of feeling my emotions, connecting with myself and looking inside – I realised the power I had within myself to change my mind and my life. *You have this in you too!* Everyone does, you just need to start with awareness, gratitude and caring! I know I'm repeating myself but this is so important to me to let you know that you have the power to change. Honestly, if I can do it, anyone can!

Even starting with something practical like a gratitude journal – can lead to change in your life and the lives of those around you. It is such a simple process and starting this process of purposely changing perspective flows on to other areas in your life.. You have the capacity to create a wonderful ripple effect around you.

Try lying in bed for a few minutes before you get up, setting good intentions for the day, feeling gratitude for the opportunities you have for that day. Even on those days where "nothing goes right" – a lot of things will go right too, you just need to notice them.

When you are feeling a bit flat, reading through your gratitude journal can help to pick you up again and set you on the right track, it can help you reset your sails.

Gratitude Meditation (Paul Bedson)

Prepare yourself for this meditation by practising mindfulness stillness based meditation for five to ten minutes.

Now bring to mind all of the material things in your life that sustain and comfort you … the food you eat, the clothes you wear, your home … Bring to mind the material things that entertain and inspire you … your books, garden, television, furnishings, artworks … In your mind, begin to recall and name all those material things. As you dwell on these things, say to yourself: Thank you. Thank you for all these things that support and comfort me, that amuse and inspire me. Thank you very much. Breathe consciously … Direct the breath towards your heart … As you breathe out, let your heart be touched with the feeling of gratitude.

Now allow to come to mind all of your teachers … all those who have encouraged, inspired or otherwise helped you to grow … Some of your teachers may have been kind, some more ruthless … In your mind, begin to recall, picture and name all of your teachers. Then say to yourself: Thank you. Thank you to all of my teachers. Thank you for the lessons you have given me. Thank you very much. Breathe consciously ... Direct the breath towards your heart ... As you breathe out, let your heart be touched with the feeling of gratitude.

Now allow to come to mind all of your friends ... all of the people who have shared fun, challenges and love with you ... all of the people who have supported you ... It may be a small select group or a larger group ... In your mind, begin to recall, picture and name all of your friends. Then say to yourself: Thank you. Thank you to all of my friends. Thank you for your love and support. Thank you very much. Breathe consciously ... Direct the breath towards your heart ... As you breathe out, let your heart be touched with the feeling of gratitude.

Now allow to come to mind all of your family members ... your parents, grandparents and ancestors who stand behind you ... your brothers and sisters who stand beside you ... perhaps your children who stand in front of you ... All of your family members ... In your mind, begin to recall, picture and bring to mind all of your family members. Then say to yourself: Thank you. Thank you to all of my family members. Thank you for all the fun, challenges and love that we have shared. Thank you for your love and support. Thank you very much. Breathe consciously ... Direct the breath towards your heart ... As you breathe out, let your heart be touched with the feeling of gratitude.

Now allow to come to mind the people with whom you have shared intimate love ... your lovers, partners, spouse ... all of the people who have touched your heart as you have touched theirs ... It may be a small select group or just one person ... In your mind, begin to recall, picture and name your beloved ones. Then say to yourself: Thank you. Thank you to my loved ones. Thank you for the love that we have shared. Thank you very much. Breathe consciously ... Direct the breath towards your heart ... As you breathe out, let your heart be touched with the feeling of gratitude.

Now bring to mind your own unique and precious self ... In your mind, begin to recall times in your life, see your face at various ages, and say your own name. Then say to yourself: Thank you. Thank you to my own true self. Thank you for this precious life. Thank you very much. Breathe consciously ... Direct the breath towards your heart ... As you breathe out, let your heart be touched with the feeling of gratitude.

Let the feeling of gratitude spread to every part of your body. Let every cell of your body say: Thank you. Thank you very much. Thank you for this unique, precious life.

If it feels appropriate, place your palms together in front of your chest in a prayer position. You may even like to bow your head a little as you continue to say to yourself and to all of Life: Thank you. Thank you very much.

Chapter 10

Your Action Plan

"It is not in the stars to hold our destiny but in ourselves."
William Shakespeare

So here we go, here's the culmination of the work you've been doing so far. Going back through your workbook or journal, you have the information required to create your action plan that will help to establish you new routines - these new processes and patterns will bring you back to you!

You see now, that no-one can give you the formula, it's a process of self-discovery that takes time to think, write and work out who you really are. This is what will bring you back to yourself – and each person's action plan will be individual, unique to them – as it should be. I have just given you questions to ponder, and a way to bring them together to create change in your life.

You were there all along! Yes, you changed through your grief and your loss but with that change comes growth, new perspective and compassion for yourself and the suffering of others. You will practice gratitude and appreciation on a daily basis, and like an echo, these wonderful feelings will return to you many times over as they are absorbed and radiated back from those around you. Most importantly, you will realise you are fundamental in the creation of your life. that innate power and strength has been there all along and you can choose to use this daily. You will create what you are committed to. And this action plan won't be the last one you create. As your life changes, you may desire more change and you will have conviction in your ability to create that change!

It is the strength of consistency and commitment that will make the change. Maybe you won't see it tomorrow or the next day, but I promise you, as you commit to yourself, you will see a change in the next few months or years, and you won't be the only one! In fact, I am suggesting that you will feel so empowered by this, that you will be encouraging those around you to do the same thing – so you will also be the catalyst for change in others. You will be changing the world around you. And you'll find the changes you make have an exponential effect rather than a linear one, all of a sudden you will reach that tipping point and find yourself experiencing joy and peace so much more than sadness and grief.

The thing you are missing the most is yourself.

Workbook Activity

So, what have you learned about yourself? This has all come to you from you working through the exercises:

1. First of all, write the heading: MY ACTION PLAN – BACK TO ME!

Underneath this write:

I love me:

So I will commit to:

Now write two things that you are going to do to show you love yourself – if you can't think of anything now, go back to some of the things your wrote earlier that are nourishing activities and use two of those. Just know that every time you commit and spend time immersed in those activities, it is an expression of self-love, a commitment to you.

2. Write your affirmations based on your commitments from above, or from ones you have written in your workbook and read them daily. Say them out loud in the first, second and third person. Make them meaningful, and mean them when you use them. They become your intention for your direction for your life. Record them on your phone, listen to them while you walk, while you drive, while you rest - whatever works best for you, but use them.
3. Commit to starting a gratitude journal or a gratitude practice

Even on your toughest days, you can still find something to be grateful for. These are the days where the biggest lessons in gratitude are learned, you find the silver lining and there always is one. You just have to make the choice to see it. Do you know how many choices you make a day – even one more stroke with the hairbrush is a choice you make – whether you are conscious of it or not, it is so. So bring more attention to yourself acting on autopilot and become involved in the direction your life is heading. Start to live your life on purpose, with purpose. Granted, you can't change everything that happens around you but you are definitely the only one who can make a choice on how to react to your world. No-one can take that from you and there is great strength in knowing that. As you commit to your gratitude journal, it will be interesting to see if your writing changes as you continue to journal. I personally have found I went from having lists or dot points, to paragraphs about what I was grateful for and why. My writing began to flow.

I must admit though that eventually my gratitude journal became a little bit of a chore – I didn't want to have to commit to expressing my gratitude that way. So there were times where it became just as easy not to do it as it was to do it, so I stopped. It became draining rather than nourishing. So while it was an integral part of establishing my gratitude practice, I write it in when I want to now. Same with my gratitude jar, when I feel moved to, I add to my jar – that way, the acknowledgement of gratitude is authentic to me.

I feel I have *become* grateful so I don't have to *do* grateful. I reflect during my day on things, events, people I am grateful for, and I often post these on Facebook. When I am in the midst of an experience of something for which I am truly grateful, I take the time to soak it up, I feel it in my body, I experience the experience of joy it brings for 10-20 seconds to embed this in my subconscious, so I can bring it back and experience it again. Express gratitude to people on a daily basis – this can be to people you don't know (for example, a shop assistant) or to people in your close circle. Very often, it's those who are closest to us that don't receive the gratitude they deserve!

4. Establish a goal – something you have always wanted to do – whether this be learning to paint, or to travel somewhere you

have always wanted to do and set a time frame for that – it doesn't have to be rigid, but make it achievable so you will do it - let it be a goal focused on joy and something you love doing. If you spend more time doing things you love, the things you were doing that were detrimental to your health or used as resistance to really feeling yourself will fall by the wayside. Your focus will change from distraction to interaction with yourself. Write this goal somewhere you can see if often, you may like to write it on a post-it note and stick it on your bathroom mirror, you might like to create a whole vision board around it, whatever takes your fancy. Let others know what your goal is and what you are working towards, they may help you stay accountable to it!

5. Meditate daily – this will restore your connection with your self and your environment and with regular practice, it will become a way of being rather than something you do. Practice with these included meditations and find if you enjoy the guided imagery meditations or the mindfulness based meditations the most, perhaps like me, you will enjoy mixing them up from time to time.

Just remember, you can let go of old beliefs that you have inherited, they were never yours in the first place! The teachers who gave them to you – your parents, teachers, employers, friends etc. did so with the best intentions and they were giving you the best of what they knew at the time. You can own your beliefs now.

This plan seems simple, and it is deliberately so. It needs to be achievable and also repeatable, so as you change and grow, you can revisit the process and extend yourself further. These are very simple techniques that you can teach others around you.

This has worked for me due to the simplicity and the ability to see the growth and change in myself. I can also practice the awareness and acceptance of where others are and let that be without judgement. People are where they are, we are not all at the same place in our journey, some won't awaken to their journeys, while others are ready to embrace it and that's okay.

Remember the things you have been successful at in your life have been things that you have committed to and practiced consistently. Maybe you were lucky, things went your way first time around but know that's not always the way. When you learned to walk as a toddler, chances are you didn't just get up on your feet and start running. You got there through "baby steps". You started by pulling yourself up on the furniture so you could stand. After a few attempts at this, you may have taken a couple of steps while holding onto the furniture. Then you found the courage to let go of the furniture and stand on your own – not ready to walk still, but you could stand alone. After multiple ups and downs, you eventually stood there and took your first step, and then the next one and within no time at all you were off. Can you imagine what life would have been like if you decided it was all too hard when you first fell on your bum when you tried to stand up? Where would you be now, what would you be doing?

Give yourself the gift of consistency, commitment and time. It won't happen immediately, you may have some lapses, which are okay, but change has to happen if you are consistently committed to it!

When you feel like you can't do it, please remember these things:

- You are worthy.

- You deserve to be happy.
- You can learn new habits and behaviours (remember how you've learned to walk, eat, talk, dress yourself, drive a car, ride a bike, run, jump – the list is endless), you just need to want to do it for yourself.

If you still feel you don't love yourself enough to commit to your plan, pretend you are doing it for someone else. Fake it until you make it! Pretend the person that you want to be is the person you are doing it for and you will deliver yourself to you. Perhaps it is the image of yourself as you are now that you don't like or are uncomfortable with, well give yourself a bloody good look in the mirror, right in your eyes and just stop and stare there. Remember yourself as a child, as a teenager, at any other important time in your life. Maybe it will help you to visualize yourself that way as you commit to your action plan. It doesn't matter what it takes to do it, just get it happening. If you've come this far through the book, you have decided you want change in your life, you have decided you are worth spending some time on, because, let's face it, this whole book has been about you. When you feel yourself straying from your plan, stop and consciously ask yourself why it's happening. Why is the resistance re-surfacing? Go back and read the resistance chapter again!

Are you afraid you won't be able to commit to change? Are you afraid to declare to someone that you are going to change? Why are you afraid? Are you afraid of failure, of what other people think, of what effect some of these changes may have in your life and on others?

Look at it from the other side and be afraid of what your life will be like if you don't make any changes – probably pretty much like it is now or worse – is that what you really want? I doubt it, because you wouldn't have started reading this book if you were happy with your life. Maybe you have a history (like me) of starting and stopping things all the time and not really knowing why you stop. Sometimes it is because it's just as easy not to do something as it is to do it. Jeff Olson talks about this in his wonderful book "The Slight Edge" and you know what, once you start to analyse your choices and make yourself make a choice, you will most likely see the value in your good choices.

That's not to say you won't fall down – and when you do, don't beat yourself up about it. Just accept that's how it is at the moment and resolve to change it tomorrow, or even right now. Accept but don't react harshly. Garner your self-compassion and self-forgiveness and you will become better at this.

You started reading this book because something needs to change and it's a bit scary starting something new sometimes. Better the devil you know you may be thinking, no No NO! You are wonderful, special and deserving of love and happiness. And you have the power to make the change; you are so much more powerful than you know. Don't be afraid of letting go of the furniture!

In *The Big Leap*, Gay Hendricks talks about our limited capacity for feeling joy. As soon as we start to feel it for too long, we turn our attention to something negative, something we can start worrying about. If we can recognize we are doing that, we can stop ourselves in our tracks and ask ourselves why we are doing it. We can let the negative go and turn our attention again to what benefits us more. It doesn't mean we ignore complications and negative issues in our lives, but we don't have to stay drowning in them like quicksand. We can navigate our way through them and return to our course.

Perhaps the simplest tool in my box is stopping myself in my tracks when I'm feeling in a funk and thinking about what I can be grateful for right now in my life. In this way I am switching from fear to love, and I allow myself to let go. This has certainly been a life changer for me. That simple act of changing my mind changes my physiology! Oh how I love to know I can do that with a thought – creating change at a cellular level! Who doesn't want that power?

This next meditation is a guided imagery where you will visualize yourself as you are now and how you want to be. This may change every time you do it, don't strive for it to be the same, to be perfect, just engage with it.

Transformation Meditation (Marion Turner)

Allow yourself to settle into your posture, hands resting in the lap, eyes gently closed, allowing your body to relax in the best way you know how, perhaps taking three slow deep conscious breaths, feeling the muscles softening and loosening on the out breath, relaxing, releasing letting go ...

Give yourself permission to be in this space, there is nothing else you need to be doing right now, nowhere else you need to be, just being here right now is perfect ...

Allow your attention to rest in the space in front of your closed eyes, this can be a focal point for stillness and observation, perhaps there are some colours or patterns here, mostly it's just dark.

Bringing your awareness to any sounds coming to you from a distance, from outside the room, noticing not judging, allowing the sounds to come and go ...

Bringing your awareness to sounds coming to you from inside the room, noticing how the sounds bring your attention to the present moment, again just observing, noticing not thinking, just awareness ...

There may be a sound associated with your breath and as you bring your attention to the breath, feel the movement associated with the breath. Feel the air moving over the nostrils, the gentle rise of the chest and the belly on the in breath, the fall on the out breath, just following each breath ...

If you find you're becoming distracted by thoughts, simply bring your attention back to the next breath and follow the breath.

Then rest your awareness on your problem, now that may be resting your awareness on how you're feeling now, how you're feeling post grief, but this could work with any problem you have. Just rest your attention there and allow the image to form as it will, don't judge, just observe with gentle curiosity, from a distance ... close by... and observing this image from different angles ...

Then imagine this image has healed, it's transformed into what you want it to be, what does it look like now? Just allow this image to form and explore this image with gentle curiosity, from a distance ... from close by ... and from different angles. And as you're observing this image, allow yourself to merge with this image and feel the feelings associated with feeling renewed and changed. What can you feel? Allow yourself to feel the healing, experience the sensations... savour the sensations ...

Compare the two images and see what has changed, it's a beginning to a new ending ... you don't need to know all the steps involved... maybe you can see a representation of what made the change ... examine this representation ...

Which of the two images is larger or more powerful to you?

Can you make the healed image larger?

Can you see the process of change? How is that happening, is it happening slowly, quickly, are there any feelings associated with this?

Feel the feelings ...

Rest your awareness on the transformation ...

Rest your awareness on the final healed image ...

Rest in this comfort ... Don't try to change the images, allow them to come to you as they come to you, resting in this peace and renewal.

Bring your awareness back to the sounds coming to you from outside the room, take a deeper breath or two, gently activate your hands and feet with a little movement, and when you are ready, gently open your eyes.

Chapter 11

Staying on Track!

"Well done is better than well said."
Benjamin Franklin

How will you stay committed to your plan? Maybe you can declare your commitment publicly on social media, or to a friend, or in a private group. Maybe you can declare your commitment to a loved one, or even to yourself. Pin it up where you can see it at home, over a mirror or two, in your bedroom, on your phone or computer as a screen saver … whatever you need to do to keep it going. I suggest you do it with someone who cares about you and your progress, maybe someone you connected with in the *From Grief to Gratitude* Facebook group or your beloved. Remember that you want to live up to what you are declaring, when you feel yourself slipping remind yourself of Benjamin Franklin's wise words.

In reality, the only person you need to commit to is yourself. The self that went missing for that period of time, look yourself in the eye in the mirror and declare your commitment.

Yes, there may be times where you don't stick to your plan. Pick yourself up, dust yourself off and get back on the wagon. Don't let that slip be your demise. It doesn't mean you have to start over, it just means you have to go back to where you got up to.

Use your self-compassion skills to accept the hiccups and definitely use them to acknowledge your steps forward. You are not perfect, nor am I, nor are any humans – except for the spiritual masters. It's okay not to be one, in fact, that's "normal". Being the best you can be is amazing, aim for that! You don't have to be the leader of the pack, but you can become the leader of you. Be a gentle guide, use love at all times, not fear. If you are getting down on yourself for stepping out of your routine – you are acting out of fear – fear of failure, fear of not being good enough, not deserving, unworthy – STOP IT! Go straight back to love, be tender, be kind. You are doing the best you can, it's okay to not be perfect, just do the best you can do. Honour your life and the lives of those around you. Don't punish yourself; you don't need to suffer to be worthy. You don't need flagellation to receive admiration; you don't need to be a martyr!

Yes there will be resistance to your practice to get back to you. We explored this in Chapter Five and you will continue to encounter resistance along your path. Simply being aware of this, being able to acknowledge and accept it for what it is and reminding yourself how to overcome this resistance will keep you moving forward. You will find other things you need to be doing instead, you will get lazy, or maybe your ego will want to make you be busy and productive and seek the approval of others.

Maybe, like me, you have a whole raft of projects that you have started and haven't finished – this can be a real emotional drain and a real distraction from committing to your action plan.

If that's the case for you, make a list of things that are important to you to get finished – and understand they won't be finished in a day, maybe they can be finished over the course of a year with a little commitment. Break them down into little tasks rather than one massive one – for example, clean out my sock drawer as opposed to de-cluttering the whole house! These small projects can probably be done in half an hour or so and it's fine to feel proud of getting some of these things off your draining list – in fact, it's nourishing when you've done so.

I have started to add to my gratitude journal by including things I have completed or accomplished at the end of the day. So some time is spent at the end of the day acknowledging myself for my commitment to get stuff done. When I don't do it that way, I tick them off my to-do list in my planner. I am very aware of the things that I put off doing, and I know that eventually these chores end up taking me hours to sort out later – such as work administration, bank reconciliations, letters and report writing, home administration, so I am aiming to not make that list grow! I congratulate myself for staying on task and getting it done. As we speak, I made sure I did the dishes and cleaned the kitchen before I sat down to write this. I am energised by having clean space around me and de-energised or drained by mess and clutter – I've had enough of that spiral. These things aren't difficult to do but they're also easy to leave for later – which is not a good choice for me!

Remember too that every day is new; every day has possibilities to behold beauty, so maybe you might like to start changing where you place your attention. If the news programs are depressing for you or they spark off negative conversations within your family environment with your loved ones complaining about politicians etc., make a choice! Make a choice not to watch it, maybe suggest no-one watches it. Maybe go for a walk instead! By the same token, don't assume everyone else in the family is committed to your growth and change either, or to their own. This is your experience and while it's nice to share some of your new perceptions and beliefs, most of those close to you, probably don't want to be taught it – not by you anyway. Teach them instead through the changes they can see in your behaviour, mood and activity.

When you feel like you are stuck in a rut, that nothing changes, know that you are not the same person you were last year, last month, last week or yesterday. You are not the same person physiologically as you were an hour ago – every second of every day some of our 35 trillion cells are going through some form of transformation – they are being killed off and replaced, they are being made healthier through the presence of different nutrients in our body. Nothing stays the same. Our thoughts, our emotions, our sensations, and our feelings constantly change, just like the sounds come and go, the clouds are different, and the bees in the garden are different. We may think everything is the same, we're still living in the same house, working the same job, driving the same car and yes that may be true. But as we engage in conversations with others, we change. Something changes within us every second of the day. We learn something from our interactions that create beliefs; we store them as memories and use them to make judgement and decisions. So, the smile you received from the receptionist at the doctor's surgery, not only created a belief about her, the effect of that smile most likely changed your experience at the surgery overall, will have altered your interaction with your doctor and so on. So you can't get away from change, and once you realize you are experiencing and coping with change constantly, you can make a choice to purposely change some of the bigger things in your life. Just do it a bit at a time. Perhaps change is the biggest constant in our lives and we have only started to become aware of that.

Dare now to let go, to let go of the safety of your habits. Create new habits that benefit you and those around you. Don't be afraid of what others may think and remember you have the right to be happy, everyone does, and doesn't feeling happy feel wonderful? Doesn't feeling peaceful feel safe? Practice experiencing the feelings, and listen to yourself.

If you feel anger, anxiety, or sadness rise up in you, stop for a moment and ask yourself why? Why are you coming from fear and not love? Is there a way to make a choice to feel different? Can you feel compassion for the person who has "made you angry" – even though it's technically *you* who "made you angry". Remember, we don't know the full story behind anyone's actions and behaviours – we may have judgement and opinions but we really don't know the truth. Heck, we're just starting to find the truth behind our own. There's a window for compassion right there – think back to how you were at the start of the book, had you even stopped to contemplate some of these things about yourself? I'm guessing maybe not, so why would everyone else have taken the time to do it? The truth is, they probably haven't, so understand that about them. Forgive them for not knowing better, for not doing better by you, for you having to take up the slack (which is also your choice).

Act out of love, so when you are taking up the slack, do it with good grace and love. I am blessed to have both my parents and my mother in law come for dinner every Thursday night. I am usually quite tired by this time of the week with work and family commitments and in the past I have found myself sometimes anticipating the event with some element of stress – I don't know what to cook, I haven't cleaned the house, the dishes aren't done etc. etc. I choose not to do that anymore. I choose to look forward to the evening, the entertainment of the conversations that come with ageing parents, the repetition of some of the conversations that come with sufferers of early dementia. I look forward to their appreciation of the dinner, the fact that we can sit and relax and chat over a meal, I don't concern myself overly much about the state of the house when they arrive, or the menu or the stage of meal preparation when they arrive. You see, it's not about that; it's about love and human connection and relationships. It's about maintaining connection with those you love when your life is a busy whirlwind. It's about prioritising things that are important to you and committing to them.

When you have strayed from your plan (that you committed too), don't be too hard on yourself. Acknowledge that you have wandered off track and gently bring yourself back to your path. Remind yourself why you are doing this, reaffirm your commitment – re-commit and get back on track. You have your affirmations you made with your plan, are you using those? Do you need a new one that is directly linked to your action plan? Maybe it could be something like this:

I "Marion Turner" am committed to reconnecting with my self and my purpose through my action plan.

Sometimes (often, I have found) we encounter resistance to change. We go along well for a few days, weeks or months, and before we know it, we've stopped doing the things that are good for us. We feel it's too hard to do our meditation, or we don't want to do it now. We can do it later (and then we don't do it at all). This can be our ego resisting change. Our ego is set to be our protector and if we are already surviving, it doesn't really like us to take a chance by changing direction. Well, we don't want to just survive; we want to thrive and really LIVE our lives. So acknowledge the ego is the resistor, I mentally thank mine for wanting the best for me, but tell it that I will listen to it occasionally, but I am connecting with my soul and my inner knowing and will continue to change to better my life.

We also need to let go of the need to control others and take control of ourselves – the one thing we can control. We can find pleasure in observing our lives around us, if only we hop down from the fence of negativity, and into the field of what "is". Things are what they are, what we make of them is up to us.

Seek the peace in your stillness, seek the gratitude in the present moment, allow, breathe and let go. You are allowed to let go. You are allowed to be happy, in fact, that is your birthright and the birthright of all human beings. Revel in the joy, the happiness, shed your tears in the sadness, share your compassion and empathy with others who are suffering, feel your feelings, but always steer your course back to joy. You are love and you are loved.

It's simple.

Postscript

When I started this book, I realized that I had not yet completed my journey (and that I may never do so) but I had no idea how much I would be continuing to go "into and through my grief". Joanne Fedler, thank you, I didn't fully understand this at the time you wrote this as you signed my copy of "Write Your Story". The meaning behind your words has become clearer with every step of this process.

Marion Turner

From Grief to Gratitude

Grief

Sits heavy on my chest

Like compressed dry earth, hard, unbreakable, unmovable

Parched by years of neglect

And then a small crack appears,

Water trickles through this crack

Slowly leaking from the inner corner of my soul

It flows upstream

Apparently the path of least resistance

And flows gently from the inner corner of my eyes

Rolls gently down my cheeks

Then "it" grabs me

Forcefully squeezes and constricts me

Until the very breath of life cannot enter my body

Then it does

With a howling in-breath

And a wracking sobbing out-breath

The cycle repeats with savage intensity

The emotion that has been denied for so long

Will be denied no more

I sit quietly now

Contemplating this eruption

The small crack that created "devastation"

Has now let the light in to my soul

I accept "it" for what it is

For what it has been

For what it has taught me

And I feel lighter,

I feel grateful, I feel love and I remember.

Marion Turner

References and further reading:

American Cancer Society. *https://www.cancer.org/treatment/end-of-life-care/grief-and-loss/depression-and-complicated-grief.html*

Brown, B. (2010). *The Gifts of Imperfection*. Center City, PA: Hazelden Information and Educational Services.

Brown, B. (2018). *Braving the Wilderness*. London, UK: Ebury Publishing.

Campbell, R. (2015). *Light is the New Black*, Carlsbad, CA: Hay House.

Cohen, A. (2015). *A Course in Miracles Made Easy*. London, UK: Hay House UK.

Dyer, W. (2007). *Inspiration: Your Ultimate Calling*. Carlsbad, CA: Hay House.

Fair Work Australia. *https://www.fairwork.gov.au/leave/compassionate-and-bereavement-leave*

Gawler, I. (2016). *The Mind that Changes Everything*, Melbourne, Vic: Brolga Publishing.

Gawler, I & Bedson, P. (2010). *Meditation: an indepth guide*. Crows Nest, NSW: Allen & Unwin.

Hanson, R. (2012). *Buddha's Brain: The Practical Neuroscience of Happiness, Love and Wisdom*. Oakland, CA: Harbinger Publications.

Hay, L. (2004). *You Can Heal Your Life*. Carlsbad, CA: Hay House Publishing.

Hendricks, G. (2011) *The Big Leap*. New York, NY: Harper Collins.

Levy, D. (2011). *Gray Matter*. Wheaton, IL: Tyndale House.

Lipton, B. (2005). *The Biology of Belief*. Carlsbad, CA: Hay House.

Neff, K. (2011). *Self-Compassion*. London, UK: Hodder & Stoughton General Division.

Olson, J. (2011.) *Slight Edge*. Austin, TX: Greenleaf Book Group.

Rossman, M. (2000). *Guided Imagery for Self-Healing.* Tiburon, CA: HJ Kramer Books.

Walsch, N. (2005). *The Complete Conversations with God: An Uncommon Dialogue*, New York, NY: Putnam Publishing.

Walsch, N. (2008). *Happier than God.* Charlottesville, VA: Hampton Roads Publishing Co.

Walsch, N. (2010). *When Everything Changes, Change Everything.* London, UK: Hodder & Stoughton General Division.

Walsch, N. (2018). *Conversations with God: Book 4. Awaken the Species, A New and Unexpected Dialogue.* London, UK: Watkins Publishing.

Zander. R. (2016). *Pathways to Possibility.* New York, NY: Penguin Putnam.

Printed in the United States
By Bookmasters